WICCA

Book of Spells
WITCHES' PLANNER 2021

*A Wheel of the Year Grimoire
with Moon Phases, Astrology,
Magical Crafts, and Magic Spells
for Wiccans and Witches*

LISA CHAMBERLAIN

DISCLAIMER

YOUR FREE GIFT

Thank you for adding this book to your Wiccan library! To learn more, why not join Lisa's Wiccan community and get an exclusive, free spell book?

The book is a great starting point for anyone looking to try their hand at practicing magic. The ten beginner-friendly spells can help you to create a positive atmosphere within your home, protect yourself from negativity, and attract love, health, and prosperity.

Little Book of Spells is now available to read on your laptop, phone, tablet, Kindle or Nook device!

To download, simply visit the following link:

www.wiccaliving.com/bonus

GET THREE
FREE AUDIOBOOKS
FROM LISA CHAMBERLAIN

Did you know that all of Lisa's books are available in audiobook format? Best of all, you can get **three audiobooks completely free** as part of a 30-day trial with Audible.

Wicca Starter Kit contains three of Lisa's most popular books for beginning Wiccans, all in one convenient place. It's the best and easiest way to learn more about Wicca while also taking audiobooks for a spin! Simply visit:

www.wiccaliving.com/free-wiccan-audiobooks

Alternatively, *Spellbook Starter Kit* is the ideal option for building your magical repertoire using candle and color magic, crystals and mineral stones, and magical herbs. Three spellbooks – over 150 spells – are available in one free volume, here:

www.wiccaliving.com/free-spell-audiobooks

Audible members receive free audiobooks every month, as well as exclusive discounts. It's a great way to experiment and see if audiobook learning works for you.

If you're not satisfied, you can cancel anytime within the trial period. You won't be charged, and you can still keep your books!

CONTENTS

INTRODUCTION

Welcome to 2021, and to the first ever *Book of Spells Witches' Planner.* This is a collaboration of contributors from many walks of Witchery, including Wicca; Traditional, Hedge, and Kitchen Witchcraft; herbalism; divination; shamanism and spirit communication; and various folk magic traditions. These writers have contributed to publications like *The Crooked Path Journal, Witch Way Magazine, Witchology Magazine,* and *Witches and Pagans Magazine,* and published books on many topics relevant to beginning and experienced Witches alike.

The spells, articles, and other gems of information within these pages are meant to help you keep your practice enlivened throughout the year. You'll find some in-depth discussions at the front of the book with a range of ideas for deepening your practice, as well as plenty of Book-of-Shadows-worthy snippets of information on crystals and herbs, magical crafts, rituals, Sabbat celebration ideas, and more – one for each week of the year.

Working with the natural timing of the Universe is a great way to enhance your magical practice, so you'll also find daily information about the phase and location of the Moon, significant astrological events like planetary retrogrades and eclipses, and, of course, the Sabbat days.

When it comes to magical timing, the phase and location of the Moon is often the most important factor. The symbols used in this planner reflect detailed tracking of the lunar cycle, and the Moon's travels through the Zodiac wheel are also noted.

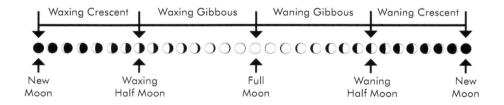

Moon ◗ enters Gemini ♊ 2:35 am

Moon ◐ v/c 6:50 am

Generally speaking, the relationship between magic and the Moon can be summed up as follows: as the Moon grows, we work magic for increase; as it wanes, we work magic for decrease. In other words, work with the waxing Moon when you want to bring something into your life, and with the waning Moon when you want to banish or release something from your experience. The Full Moon – the halfway point in the lunar cycle – is a time for appreciating and celebrating our manifestations and achievements, while the New Moon – the beginning of the cycle – is ideal for setting new intentions.

The location of the Moon, or the Zodiac sign it's traveling through at any given moment, can also be significant in terms of magical timing. Different signs are ideal for different magical purposes, which are detailed on pages 10 and 11. Some Witches find that working when the Moon is void-of-course ("v/c"), or in between one sign and the next, leads to less effective magic, while others experience no difficulty with spells cast at these times. You may want to experiment with this, and see what works best for you.

It's important to note that this planner uses U.S. Eastern Standard Time/ Eastern Daylight Time (depending on which is applicable), so if you live in a different time zone, you'll need to calculate the difference in the hours noted for astrological events. This also means that certain dates may be slightly off, depending on where you live. You can find plenty of time zone converters online to help you make the needed adjustments.

Finally, because the contributors represent such a wide spectrum of magical backgrounds and perspectives on the Craft, you may notice some inconsistencies in the spelling and capitalization of certain terms, as well as a variety of magical terminology. This is to be expected, given the rich diversity of paths within the Witching world, and these differences are celebrated here.

I and the other authors of this book hope you will find it a fun and useful way to integrate magic and Witchcraft into your days in 2021. May you have an incredibly blessed and magical year!

– Lisa Chamberlain

ZODIAC SIGNS AND MAGICAL PURPOSES

Moon in Zodiac sign	Work magic related to...
Aries	new ventures, general health and vitality, self-improvement, difficult conflicts, navigating issues with bureaucracy, leadership, authority, impatience difficult tempers, surgery
Taurus	money, prosperity, real estate, material acquisitions, self-esteem, love, sensuality, gardening and farming, fertility, patience, endurance, commitment, music, the arts, business
Gemini	intelligence, communication, commerce, siblings, writing, teaching, neighbors, dealing with gossip, travel, transportation, public relations, media, networking, adaptability, memory, LGBT issues
Cancer	home, family, mothers, children, traditions, weather and climate, security, integrity, water issues (particularly natural bodies of water), psychic abilities, integrity, listening to and assisting others
Leo	love (platonic), self-confidence, self-expression, performing in public, vacation and leisure time, courage, childbirth, taking risks, good cheer, gambling, amusement, creativity, loyalty, fine arts
Virgo	health and healing, diet, business and trade, tools, employment, intelligence and intellect, co-workers, military and police, exercise and fitness, work ethic, debt, cleansing and purification, hunting, pets

Moon in Zodiac sign	Work magic related to...
Libra	legal matters, justice, marriage, peace, balance, diplomacy, beauty, harmony, team-building, contracts, romance and dating, partnership, art and music, socializing, meeting people, overcoming laziness
Scorpio	regeneration, renewal, sex, death, secrets, divination, psychic development, banishing, willpower, purification, hypnotism, emotional honesty, solitude, courage, transformation, mediumship
Sagittarius	optimism, resilience, generosity, legal matters, education (especially higher education), ethics, dreams, contacting the divine, generosity, fame, publishing, good luck, long journeys, fun, humor, languages
Capricorn	careers, jobs, promotions, fathers, responsibility, solitude, healing from depression, ambition, public recognition, honor, reputation, awards, long term results, government, time management, wisdom,
Aquarius	friendship, acquaintances, politics, electronics, freedom, science, extrasensory development, breaking bad habits, problem solving, objectivity, luck, meeting new people, social justice, hope
Pisces	psychic ability, music, spirituality, criminal matters, widows and orphans, reversing bad luck, finding lost items, charity, self-reflection, past lives, facing fears, endings, water (particularly oceans and salt water), dance, drug and alcohol problems

SABBATS OF 2021

(Sabbath - gathering)

Imbolc	February 2 *Mark beginning of spring* *Imbolc cross-quarter day February 3
Ostara	March 20 *Goddess of spring and dawn.*
Beltane	May 1 *Halfway between spring equinox and summer solstice.* *Beltane cross-quarter day May 5
Litha	June 20 *Summer solstice. Beginning of summer.*
Lammas	August 1 *Harvest festival* *Lammas cross-quarter day August 7
Mabon	September 22 *Wheel of the year. Celebrate continuous turning of time and mirrors natures cycles of *
Samhain	October 31 *Marking the end of the summer and beginning of winter. ⊕* *Samhain cross-quarter day November 6
Yule	December 21 *Eternal cycle of life and death. Battle between light & dark. Hope the sun will return.*

Halfway between winter solstice and spring equinox.

* *Death and rebirth.*
⊕ *The darker half of the year.*

FULL MOONS OF 2021

Wolf Moon	January 28	2:16 pm	7.16
Snow Moon	February 27 ✳	3:17 am	8.17
Storm Moon	March 28	2:48 pm	7.48
Pink Moon	April 26 ✳	11:31 pm	4.30
Flower Moon	May 26	7:14 am	12.14
Strawberry Moon	June 24	2:40 pm	7.40
Thunder Moon	July 23 ✳	10:37 pm	3:37
Corn Moon (*Blue Moon)	August 22	8:02 am	1.02
Harvest Moon	September 20 ✳	7:55 pm	12.55
Hunter's Moon	October 20	10:57 am	4.57
Frost Moon	November 19 ✳	3:57 am	8.57
Long Nights Moon	December 18 ✳	11:35 pm	4.35

✳ A.M in the UK

Using time converter from U.S. Eastern
Standard Time to U.K time.

ECLIPSES OF 2021

Date	Eclipse Type	Time	Zodiac Sign & Degree
May 26	Total Lunar Eclipse	7:14 am	5° Sagittarius♐ 26'
June 10	Annular Solar Eclipse	6:52 am	19° Gemini♊ 47'
November 19	Partial Lunar Eclipse	3:57 am	27° Taurus♉ 14'
December 4	Total Solar Eclipse	2:43 am	12° Sagittarius♐ 22'

PLANETARY RETROGRADES OF 2021

Planet	Date and Time Retrograde	Date and Time Direct
Uranus ♅	August 15 (2020), 10:27 am	January 14, 3:36 am
Mercury ☿	January 30, 10:51 am	February 20, 7:52 pm
Pluto ♇	April 27, 4:02 pm	October 6, 2:29 pm
Saturn ♄	May 23, 5:09 am	October 10, 10:17 pm
Mercury ☿	May 29, 6:34 pm	June 22, 6:00 pm
Jupiter ♃	June 20, 11:05 am	October 18, 1:30 am
Neptune ♆	June 25, 3:21 pm	December 1, 8:22 am
Uranus ♅	August 19, 9:40 pm ·	January 18 (2022), 10:26 am
Mercury ☿	September 27, 1:10 am	October 18, 11:17 am
Venus ♀	December 19, 5:36 am	January 29 (2022), 3:46 am

MAGICAL EMPOWERMENT FOR INTERESTING TIMES

Unless you just showed up on planet Earth yesterday, you'll have noticed that we are living, to put it mildly, in interesting times. The past year saw an unprecedented amount of upheaval, as events unfolded that ultimately affected every country, and arguably every person, on the planet. Daily life for hundreds of millions was completely upended. As a result, many people around the world have struggled with feelings of fear, helplessness, despair, and frustration, including plenty of Witches.

It's understandable to have negative reactions to such chaotic times. But letting such feelings dominate our outlook on the world presents a specific problem for Witches:

You cannot work successful magic from a place of disempowerment.

We know that like attracts like, that everything and every person vibrates with energy, and that our focused intentions are what determine the results of our magic. If you're casting spells while you're in a bad mood, or feeling frightened, or heartbroken, or any other negative emotion, those energies will almost certainly be reflected in the manifestations you bring forth. This is why it's so important to get in the right state of mind before spellwork, and to have strategies for doing so – whether it's meditation, visualization, a ritual bath, casting a circle, raising power, or all of the above.

That state of mind – in which we know we are powerful and can manifest our focused intentions – is what empowerment feels like, and it doesn't have to be reserved just for ritual occasions and spellwork. When you connect with your magical self on a daily basis, you can stay more consistently in a place of balance, ease, and trust in your own personal life journey, no matter what's happening in the world around you. And of course, feeling empowered more consistently makes it easier to get into the magical mind frame needed for successful spellwork – that's simple Law of Attraction!

So how can you maintain a stronger sense of empowerment in a messy, unpredictable, and sometimes-scary world?

Daily Magical Habits for Inner Balance and Peace of Mind

If you don't already have a daily ritual that puts you in touch with your spiritual, magical self, establish one now. No matter how simple or brief, these daily moments help us stay more consistently in our own individual energetic flow, regardless of what's happening in the external world. Try one or more of the following suggestions, or create your own for your unique practice.

Morning Tea Ritual

Create a magical morning tea blend with herbs that promote balance, tranquility, and positive energy. Many herbs have adaptogenic properties, meaning they help your body deal with stress. Herbs are also great for calming the nerves and assisting with mental clarity, without any side effects of caffeine. (But you can always have your morning coffee after your tea, if you wish!) Some delightful magical herbs to choose from include ashwagandha, chamomile, ginger, ginkgo, hibiscus, nettles, and peppermint. Light a tea light candle as your brew steeps, and envision the charged tea infusing you with calm, centered, joyful energy that lasts throughout the day.

Journaling

Designate a time during the day (perhaps while enjoying your magical tea) to spend at least ten minutes writing in a journal, your Book of Shadows, or even in a notebook just for the purpose of this activity. You can simply write stream-of-consciousness style, just to clear out any cobwebs from the mind. You can also set intentions for your day, brainstorm about magical goals, mull over a decision you need to make, or even write some poetry. The content isn't as important as the grounding and centering that a consistent journaling practice can provide.

Daily Crystals

Keep a collection of small crystals charged and ready for this purpose. At the start of each day, choose a crystal (or two!) to keep with you throughout the day, whether in a pocket or purse, on a cord, or somewhere in your home or office designated to displaying the chosen stone. Let your intuition guide your selection each day – your stones will work with you to help you choose the one with the most beneficial energy for you in the moment. Good crystals for balance, stability, and positive vibrations include amethyst, bloodstone, carnelian, citrine, clear quartz, jade, rose quartz, and smoky quartz.

Evening Peace Ritual

As you wind down from your day, light a candle with the intention of harnessing the energies of peace and harmony. Connect with these energies within yourself, and then visualize them radiating outward into the world. You can anoint your candle with a magical oil blend charged for peace, and/or burn sage or palo santo to enhance the work.

Meditation

If you don't meditate regularly (or at all), there's no time like the present to take up the practice. Even 5 minutes of daily meditation (but ideally 15 to 20 minutes) makes a significant difference in your ability to stay centered in difficult situations. Of course, it's also a powerful way to prepare for magic!

Magical Citizenship on Planet Earth

Focusing inward, through meditating, journaling, candle rituals, and other personalized practices, is important work. In fact, it's necessary for maintaining balance, tranquility, and authentic self-empowerment. Yet most of us don't get to live like hermits on a mountaintop for any length of time. We live in the world with everyone else, and most of us are constantly bombarded with reminders of that fact!

So how can we stay magically empowered while still participating in a topsy-turvy world? This is ultimately up to each person, but here are a few easy ways to find and maintain your balance:

Take social media breaks. We've all heard the saying "you are what you eat," but you also are what you read, watch, think about, and engage with. Take note of how you feel after getting online. If it isn't a positive feeling, put the device down and focus your attention elsewhere.

Then, once you get back on your favorite platform, start changing the way you use it. Stay out of arguments and debates for awhile. Don't pay attention to more negative news than is necessary. Find positive developments to share, and get in the habit of focusing on what's going well. Cultivate a positive social media feed that promotes good news, inspiring quotes, and humor. Remember that the people you share these things with will benefit from their energy.

Read astrology blogs. Find some astrologers you resonate with and follow them for help contextualizing world events. When you can start seeing issues and events as interesting from an astrological viewpoint, rather than merely chaotic or upsetting, you are maintaining an empowered observer's perspective on the world around you. This helps you stay out of helplessness and fear.

Remember the power of collective intention. The Sabbats are often referred to as "days of power." This is partly because of their positioning within the solar year, but also because so many people around the world are performing rituals and working magic at these times, as has been done for thousands of years. So these are great times to contribute your energy to positive magic for the good of the planet.

But also keep in mind that as humans, our collective consciousness affects the physical reality of Earth every day, not just on Sabbat days. This means that literally every moment is an opportunity to intend for positive outcomes in the world, rather than focusing on what seems to be going wrong. So what does your ideal world look like? Peace, freedom, prosperity and justice for all? A universal commitment to healing the Earth? An end to poverty? Whatever it is you wish to see, hold the vision of it and look for glimpses of it in your daily life – no matter how seemingly insignificant. Use that Law of Attraction to your advantage, for yourself and for the world.

As we enter 2021, I hope you will enjoy being empowered in your own unique, beautifully magical way. Blessed Be!

– Lisa Chamberlain

DIVINATION FOR THE WHEEL OF THE YEAR

While divination is a year-round activity, it can be a fun tradition to perform special types of divination at each of the Sabbats. Here we will examine unique approaches to divination that celebrate and honor the themes and energies of each of the eight major holidays.

Samhain is considered a powerful time to practice all types of divination. That being said, divination using apples is particularly appropriate for this sabbat. For matters of love, peel an apple in a circular motion, trying to create one long, continuous piece of peel. Then take the peel and throw it over your left shoulder. Examine the shape the peel makes on the ground, looking to see what letter it most resembles. This letter will be an initial of your future love interest.

Or, cut an apple and half and count the seeds. If there are an even number of seeds, marriage is in the near future. If there are an odd number of seeds, you may be single for a while longer.

While it is cold outside at **Yule** and you are cozy inside, consider trying bibliomancy, which is divination with books. Find a book you are drawn to and hold it in your hands. Close your eyes and ask a question in your mind, concentrating on the question for a moment. Open your eyes, and slowly open the book, allowing it to naturally open where it pleases. Read the first passage that captures your eye to see the answer to your question.

To honor of Brigid's holiday at **Imbolc**, take inspiration from her eternal flame and try divination with candles. Light a candle and allow it to burn long enough to melt some wax. While watching the flame, notice the height of the flame – if it is high then you have good outcomes on the way. A flickering flame could indicate change. Once you have liquid wax, carefully pour the wax into a glass of water. Examine the shape of the wax and see if you recognize any objects or images.

At the fertile holiday of **Ostara**, many people revere the symbol of the egg. At this time, try oomancy, or divination with eggs. Boil water in a large saucepan. Pour an egg white into the boiling water. Interpret the shapes you see in the eggs for any messages or predictions.

While enjoying the vibrant energy of growth and beauty of life at **Beltane**, try floromancy, or divination with flowers. One method is to go on a solitary walk in the woods or in a meadow. Note the very first flower you see, and use this as a means of divination. For example, if you see a yellow flower first, this could indicate a time of success. A white flower may indicate a time of hope and new beginnings. You can also read about the folklore of the flower you discovered for further potential messages.

If you have to make a choice between two options, harvest or buy two roses. Define the first rose as one option, and the second rose as your other option. Set them both in a vase in the sunlight. The one that blooms and lasts longer is the better option, while the one that stays closed or withers first is not the best choice.

When the sun as at its strongest at **Litha**, enjoy the outdoors at while trying nephomancy, or cloud divination. Examine the clouds and watch for shapes you recognize, noting your sixth-sense reactions to these shapes. What information is being communicated here? Clouds quickly changing shape indicate unexpected events. Clouds moving rapidly across the sky indicate transition, while stagnant clouds can indicate a pause in action. Dark clouds are typically a negative omen, while bright clouds are a positive omen.

Lughnasadh's traditions include games and friendly competitions. To test your luck on Lughnasadh, try cleromancy, which is divination with dice. There are many different ways to interpret answers from dice. One of the simplest ways is to ask a question that will have a "yes" or "no" answer. If you roll an odd number on the dice, your answer is "yes." If you roll an even number on the dice, your answer is "no."

To honor the theme of balance at the equinox, try using a pendulum to divine at **Mabon**. A pendulum can be any weighted object on a string (the most common modern version is a crystal point on a chain). Hold the tip of the chain with so the pendulum remains stationary. Then, ask the pendulum to show you "yes." It should start moving, possibly sideways, up and down, or clockwise. Next, ask the pendulum to show you "no." It should move in a distinctly different fashion. When you feel familiar with how your pendulum moves, you can start asking it questions.

If you enjoy divination, take advantage of the energies at each Sabbat to ask about your desires, goals, and spiritual progress for the current year. If you read tarot or oracle cards, consider using a Sabbat-themed spread. Enjoy the practice of divination as a way to track your successes, recognize new opportunities, and support spiritual development.

– Kiki Dombrowski

THE MAGICKAL PANTRY

In today's world we have access to such wondrous and fantastical herbs, roots, minerals, and curios to work our magic with. The internet connects us to many corners of the globe and all manner of exotic-sounding ingredients to add to our magical apothecaries. However in times past, our ancestors did not have this luxury. Often, they would have to work with what they had on hand, or what they could source from the land around them – and they had to make it last until the next harvest.

These days we are much luckier, but as a result, we've lost something of our folk magic roots – an appreciation for working with what's near at hand to boost our workings and add value to our practice. We often do not think of our humble pantry as the door to wondrous workings, but with a little imagination and appreciation for the ingredients that live within, we can uncover a whole world of amazing items to use.

Kitchen witches know the magic of ingredients that can be found in the home. Your pantry can offer such amazing options, and often the most simple ingredient can pack the biggest magical punch. For example, let's have a look at basic spice mixes you may have in your kitchen. Most mixed herb blends come with parsley, rosemary, sage, thyme and basil – a perfectly good protection blend. Pumpkin spice comes with cinnamon, clove, nutmeg, ginger and allspice – a ready-at-hand money incense blend.

Your spice blends could easily be steeped in ordinary cooking oil to create a quick magical oil, or sprinkled about the home as a floor sweep. Or, simply bless them to their magical purpose when adding them to your food, so that you ingest the spirit of the herbs and the intent of the magic.

If you want to be environmentally friendly when casting circle or creating sigils outside, corn flour is a biodegradable and non-harmful alternative to chalk or salt. It sticks to the ground so that you can see your outline, but it also easily washes away and breaks down so as not to damage the environment around you. Don't have corn flour? Plain old normal flour will do in a pinch.

Here are just a few magical goals you can create recipes and spells for, right out of your kitchen:

- **Protection:** Anise, barley, bay, chilli, caraway, cloves, cumin, dill, garlic, marjoram, onion, pepper

Protection magic is a must in any witch's arsenal, whatever path you practice. As witches walking the different worlds, we often come across and have attach to us different sorts of energies and spirits, so protection is an important skill to learn. Using herbs, grains, and vegetables, you will be able to craft powders, oils, incenses, and meals that correspond to protective energies.

- **Prosperity:** Allspice, basil, cinnamon, clove, dill, fenugreek, ginger, marjoram, mint, oats, tea

Let's be honest, when finances are flowing, things are much easier, and life is a little bit less stressful. Money magic is probably one of the oldest types of magic – since the dawn of trade humans have needed to have goods or coin in order to get what they require. The above herbs and spices are excellent for working some money magic.

- **Love:** Apple, basil, cardamom, clove, coriander, dill, ginger, lavender, lime, marjoram, rosemary, vanilla

Love is another highly explored branch of magic – in one way or another, we all want love and affection in our lives. While the more popular herbs such Rose, Hibiscus, Jasmine and Damiana are more traditionally used in love magic, the humble pantry offers up a tantalizing set of options as well.

A few more folk magic practices using common pantry items:

- **Sweetening magic:** caster sugar, honey, maple syrup, sweetener, vanilla
- **Hot magic:** cayenne pepper, cajun seasoning, chili, black pepper, mustard, ginger
- **Divination:** coffee grounds, tea leaves, bay, celery, lemongrass, saffron, thyme
- **Candle magic:** birthday candles, tea lights, dinner tapers

Quick Pantry Lucky Rice

A very quick recipe that can be comprised entirely of items from your kitchen pantry is Lucky Rice – a traditional hoodoo formula for bringing in wealth and prosperity. The wonderful thing about Lucky Rice is that it can be added to money jars and charm bags, sprinkled under your door, and used in any money or wealth workings. It's very simple, very easy to make and – once empowered with your intention and words – a powerful magical tool to use.

You will need:

- ½ cup white rice
- ½ tsp pumpkin spice
- ½ tsp marjoram
- Green food coloring
- 1 tsp basil

Instructions:

1. Mix in a small amount of green food coloring into the white rice.
2. Allow to dry overnight.
3. Add your herbs and spices to the colored rice and mix thoroughly.
4. Pour into an airtight jar or ziplock bag.

As you can see, the pantry offers up a wealth of different options for you to work your magic with. This is just an outline of what is possible, so go on, head into your kitchen, take stock of what you have at hand, and see what magic you can rustle up with just your magical pantry!

– *Stacey Carroll*

A PLANTING SPELL FOR PERSONAL GROWTH

Growth is needed when there is a desire to empower yourself and create positive change in your life. Growth can also help you get more out of life, become more compassionate, discover your full potential, and move forward emotionally and psychologically. The benefits of growth can be seen in any areas of your life, internally and externally – in business, career, love, family relationships, and even psychic and magical abilities.

A planting spell that works with actual plants is a great way to harness the natural growth energies of the spring (or summer) season, and manifest your intentions and desires. Just as the seeds begin to grow, so do your intentions. The key to this spell will be in your mindset and what you want to grow.

There are a couple of different ways you can begin this spell. My favorite way is to germinate a few seeds in an egg carton. These are easy to use, lightweight, and sized well to hold just enough soil. For those new to gardening (and even for seasoned gardeners), it can be difficult to sow seeds directly, as many don't survive, and weeds can interfere and absorb the nutrients. The egg carton gives you something of a more controlled head start.

If starting from seeds just seems too tricky or intimidating, you can always work with a young plant start that's already in a pot. Try your favorite culinary herb from the supermarket. These are highly rewarding to grow, as you can use them for a bit of kitchen witchery once they're big enough to be harvested.

You may also already have some plants in your home. If so, this is a good time for pruning, shaping, and repotting one or more plants into a larger container. Whichever approach you choose will be a great way to work with growth and life and weave your intentions into the season.

The method described here is the egg carton seeding, as this method starts from very little. Repurposing egg cartons will cost you nothing and is great for first-timers or even performing this with your children. Starting seeds in a controlled, indoor environment ensures a stronger start as the weather isn't an issue. Seeds that are great to get started are medicinal and culinary herbs. Popular choices that grow easily from a seed include basil, calendula, cilantro, dill, oregano, parsley, sage, and thyme.

For the successful growth of seeds, you'll want to follow the seed packets' directions regarding sunlight and watering. After the spell has begun, you'll be rewarded with the growth of your seeds and your intentions.

You will need:

- 6 or 12 slot cardboard egg carton
- Potting soil
- Waterproof tray or plate
- Green candle (optional)
- Scissors or a sharp knife
- Seeds of your choice
- Spray bottle with water

Instructions:

Gather your materials and prepare your workspace. Start your seeds off on the right foot by creating a cleansed and safe environment. You may want to clear away old energies through smudging, asperging, or visualization. Light a green candle for added energies of luck, fertility, growth, and prosperity. Candles are an excellent way to boost energy during magical workings. Set your intentions for all that you want to achieve and grow.

Begin crafting your egg carton by placing it on your waterproof tray, cutting off the lid, and poking small holes in the bottom of each egg cavity for drainage. Fill each egg slot with potting soil and use your finger to create a hole in each one. Place a seed in each slot and cover them with soil. If you are planting larger plants such as vegetables, one should be enough. If you are planting smaller herbs, you can add 3-4 seeds.

To raise energy, say the incantation:

"Little seeds, infuse with the energy of spring to sprout and grow."

Spray the soil with water. Keep the egg carton in a warm, light-filled location indoors until the seeds begin to sprout. Once the sprouting has begun, you can place them in their permanent home. If moving them outdoors, dig small holes and place the egg carton cups directly in the soil. They will decompose. Repeat the incantation when securing the seedlings in their new home.

Water your plants regularly and take note of their growth, remembering that they started out as tiny seeds. Enjoy the reward that comes with planting seeds and starting new life. It's the first step to a fruitful harvest.

– Severina Sosa

GENIUS LOCI

Genius loci (plural genii locorum) comes from the Latin words genius, meaning "spirit outside of the human body," and loci, meaning "place," thus literally translating to "spirit of place." Genii locorum can be found in a number of cultures around the world and some sources suggest that many deities worshiped historically and today originated from local spirits of place who became such a cultural foundation that they rose above the status of genius loci. Either way, working with your local genius loci is a critical component of natural, local witchcraft.

Generally these local spirits are protective in nature, inhabiting anything from a rock to a small patch of woods to an entire city. While they may manifest in a form we can see, they are more often invisible to the naked eye, forcing us to rely on our other senses to detect and work with them. Depending on the area where they dwell, these spirits may be extremely hesitant to work with you, especially if it's an area that has been highly disturbed by humans. Just as with any living creature, they are easily upset by unwelcome guests and destruction of their home. Spirits in areas that have been heavily influenced by humans are going to be harder to reach and work with than those in areas left generally undisturbed. However, that doesn't mean living in a city or highly developed area makes contact with your local spirits impossible.

During the Spring and Summer, most genii locorum are highly active, just like plants and animals, making these months the perfect time to try and connect with your local spirits. Once you have established a relationship with your local spirits, it is likely they will prove to be valuable allies, as they know the plants, animals, rocks, and liminal places within an area better than any other living creature.

To begin building a relationship with your local spirits, you must first venture outside. Spend time in nature, quietly taking in the world around you. Meditate and reach your energy out, looking for other energetic sources in the immediate area. Make it known that you wish to connect with the local spirits, whether out loud or in your mind, but do not expect an immediate response. Remember, many of these spirits are untrusting of humans, and you will need to spend time building relationships and proving your worth before they will make themselves known to you. But how exactly can you prove your worth to the local spirits?

1. **Be respectful.** This is one of the most important steps when it comes to gaining the trust of local spirits. When you are in their home, be mindful of how you are treating it. Stick to animal paths. Avoid littering and taking whatever you want without asking and without payment. You are trying to show the spirits that you care as much about their home as they do. Showing respect to their home sets you apart from other humans they may have encountered. When they do finally reach out to you, treat them with respect as well. If they ask something of you, honor their request the best you can, and never demand they work for you. You are in their home, so act like it.

2. **Pick up litter.** While traversing the land, pick up any litter you may find in the area. Even in the most wild of areas, litter always seems to find its way in, traveling via air and water. The spirits will notice you tending to their home and will be appreciative of it.

3. **Leave eco-friendly offerings.** Spirits love gifts, especially when they are eco-friendly. Local crystals, food, and libations are excellent gifts to offer local spirits, but be mindful of the possible impacts of these gifts. Do not bring any foods that may harm local wildlife. Bring an offering each time you visit the area to show the local spirits you respect them and care for them.

4. **Grow native plants.** If you happen to garden, be mindful of the plants you are growing. Many of the beautiful flowers found at your local nursery are not local and many more are extremely invasive. Pick plants from your area or those that are non-invasive and will provide local pollinators with food. Avoid synthetic pesticides, weed killers, and fertilizers as these runoff into local rivers and streams and can poison the soil. Nothing shows your disrespect of local spirits more than polluting the land.

5. **Be patient.** It will take time for the spirits to trust you and reach out to you. Let it be on their terms.

Each local spirit is unique, as is each relationship between human and spirit. The best way to learn about the genii locorum near you is to begin to respectfully connect with them. Once a relationship is formed, they will be happy to help in your magical workings.

– Autumn Willow

FLYING OINTMENTS: FACT OR FICTION?

The use of ointments to aid witches in their bidding dates to antiquity and is the subject of much lore and controversy. It's also a common part of the age-old perception of witchcraft as a dark practice, since these ointments are composed of poisonous herbs. Even Shakespeare associated witches with toxic plants, and the Romans believed witches anointed themselves with oil in order to shapeshift and fly. But the actual history and use of flying ointments is a little less sexy.

Flying ointments' rich history and complex social, political and religious contexts makes them ripe for study. Indeed, many have written about the interweaving of these influences as they relate to flying ointments. This fascination has resulted in a lot of information, spanning thousands of years, and it's a little hard to condense.

The lore of witches and their "flying" habits often points to the use of some kind of ointment, the ingredients of which often vary, which allowed them to fly, either physically or psychically. These ointments were said to consist of some sort of fat from children or animals, and usually included toxic or hallucinogenic herbs, soot, blood and parsley – an herb that resembles poison-hemlock.

The continued appearance of flying ointments in historical documents, dating from the Roman era into medieval times and even up to the 1940s, suggests to some that flying ointments did exist, but this can't be guaranteed. It's also possible these references were based on made-up tales. Flying ointment recipes would have been passed from witch to witch, and to have such a rich oral-only tradition handed down intact through so many generations would be a tremendous feat.

Scholars have suggested that flying ointments were a concoction of society as a way to rationalize the belief that witches appeared in places they were not or could not be present, and to explain how they performed the devil's bidding. The ointment was said to come from the devil himself and was rubbed on the witch and on any flying tool (typically, a broom). These witches then physically flew to their destination. It's important to note the belief in physical flying, since it was thought that if witches were "flying" only in their minds, they could not be guilty of the crimes they were being accused of.

The use of oils, herbs, and beeswax blended into a topical healing aid was a long-practiced tradition among even laymen, when physicians were too expensive and rare to access. Most individuals had to rely on apothecaries or personal gardens for herbal healing. Given this common practice in the days of witchcraft hysteria, it only made sense that topical ointments would come to be associated with nefarious deeds.

Some suggest that these ointments included psychoactive ingredients, which caused the witch to imagine flight. This would lend support to the argument that the ointments did exist, as certain hallucinogenic herbs were typically listed as flying ointment ingredients. However, these herbs, like belladonna and hemlock, were also terribly toxic, and would have certainly caused death. A witch who knew this would not have rubbed it on the skin.

What's more, many other herbs listed, like aconite, are not intensely hallucinogenic in nature, while herbs that are considered hallucinogenic (namely mandrake) were not included in recipes that were supposedly actually used. What this suggests is that "flying ointment" is part of a lore that associates witches with ill-intention and death, rather than an actual ointment used to promote astral projection and the feeling of flying. Nonetheless, in some cases, medieval "recipes" that have been tested did yield psychedelic experiences that included flying, which again supports the possibility that these ointments were real.

While this critical look into flying ointments is less exciting than the lore, the appeal of ointments prevails, and they are commonly used in modern witchcraft practice. We can craft ointments using the same basic structure of 90% liquid, 10% solid base (like beeswax), and then adding herbs and essential oils as desired.

To Make Flying Ointment

For a safe ointment that pays homage to this lore but also carries magical properties of protection, combine 1 cup coconut oil (or any favorite oil) and a hardy pinch of dried – not fresh – mugwort, lavender, parsley and rosemary. Add a pinch of black pepper. Let this stew on low heat for thirty minutes. To this liquid, add in beeswax or beeswax pastilles. Continue to test the consistency by allowing the solids to melt, drawing a teaspoon and letting it solidify. If the consistency is too stiff, add a little more oil. If it's too greasy for your liking, add in a pinch more beeswax. As with many concoctions, ointment consistency is a personal preference.

When you've reached the desired consistency, add in a few drops of pine, lavender or sandalwood oil and lower the temperature of the mixture to "low." Pour into opaque glass containers slowly, often pausing between layers to limit air bubbles. When all has solidified, place a piece of an herb of your choosing at the top. Apply on the skin when performing protective work.

– Sarah Justice

POST SPELLWORK FATIGUE

Allow me to set the mood for you:

You just finished casting a critical spell. You did everything you needed and wanted to do, and you can feel it! Deep within your bones, the prickling, tingling, and pulsing energy you raised is evident. There is an unmistakable power within you, around you, and part of you! It feels amazing! There is no doubt your spell will manifest, and this excites you even more. You can't contain yourself. You feel like you just drank an entire pot of coffee. Your body and mind are moving a mile a minute. You feel the blood rushing through your veins, and your heart is about to jump out of your chest! You connected with something much bigger than you, and it ignited something fantastic. Magick is most assuredly afoot!

If you have done workings where you hit that sweet in raising energy, you know this power and the elation that comes with it. It starts with a euphoric sensation that tingles and flows through the body. It's an unmistakable rush of pure cosmic energy! You did it!

Witches everywhere yearn for this sensation. This excellent feeling is confirmation that all your hard work will not be wasted. With any luck, this surge of energy might last long enough to add some momentum for your task list!

But this incredible energy can come with a severe downside. As we come down from this energetic high, we can experience many adverse effects – like headaches, severe fatigue, brain fog, and even nausea. This is where balance needs to be established. Too much of anything is not suitable for any of us.

I have experienced the human side effects of raising powerful energy and remaining in the direct presence of Divine power for too long. Often the ill effects and feelings only last a few hours, but there are no guarantees. I remember an instance when I was down and out for days. I was relatively new to the path, and I had not yet grasped the methods of dealing with significant amounts of energy. At the time, I was attending an intensive spiritual retreat. We spent the entire weekend shoulder-deep in spiritual lessons and activities. After attending a workshop teaching us how to raise and direct energy, I was on fire! My body tingled, and my mind was racing. This was the best feeling ever... until I crashed.

I thought I was doing enough to center and ground out this energy, but it was just too much. At the time, I did not have a teacher or mentor to help me through it. Suddenly, I was struggling with nausea, headaches, body aches, and severe fatigue. To make things worse, the long weekend was over, and I had to return to the mundane world. It was unbearable having to drag myself out of bed and into the office, when I felt like I had been run over by a truck.

Too much intense spiritual energy can deplete you on many levels. Your body may feel the sudden slump in energy and react accordingly. This slump can also cause an emotional upheaval. The critical thing to remember as a Witch is that you need to take care of yourself. I hope you find the following tips helpful:

- **Ground and center.** Learning to center and ground out energy will help you come back into balance much more quickly. This practice is an essential skill to develop.

- **Eat something.** Many Witches swear by eating carbs (or rather sweets) and bread. In my experience, this makes me feel worse. I do much better with fresh whole foods - like lean protein, fresh fruits, and vegetables.

- **Drink plenty of water & tea.** Remaining hydrated is essential when we want to come back into balance. Water and quality teas will help you hydrate and reclaim your balanced state. Drinking herbal teas blended with adaptogenic and anti-inflammatory herbs (like nettle and rosehips) may prove exceptionally useful.

- **Rest.** I am not a napper, but I have learned the value of taking a good nap after I raise significant amounts of energy. Allowing the body to rest and recharge is never a bad idea.

- **Connect with your Guides.** Spend some time in prayer or meditation as you connect with your guides, asking for their wisdom. Prepare yourself to communicate with them about the direction you should take and the tasks you must complete. Sometimes you will not be able to rest until this is done.

- **Reiki or other energy healing.** Seeking the help of Witches who practice energy balancing and healing can make a huge difference in your recovery.

I hope you have great success with these methods!

– Leandra Witchwood

TRIPLE GODDESS MEDITATION

The Triple Goddess is a goddess with three distinct aspects: Maiden, Mother, and Crone. She's a diverse deity whose aspects can also correspond to phases of the moon. The Triple Goddess can be thought of as a single deity with three aspects, but she can also be comprised of three different deities. For example, Greek goddesses that are often considered to be part of the Triple Goddess are Artemis as the Maiden, Selene as the Mother, and Hecate as the Crone. However you choose to work with this triple deity, she has the ability to help you through beginnings and endings; birth, death, and rebirth; inner growth; the four seasons; the lunar cycle; and the stages of your own life cycle. You can connect with the Triple Goddess in one form or all three. The choice is yours.

Meditation is a great way to connect with the Triple Goddess in all or one of her aspects. Her guidance can support and assist you with attuning your energy, focusing your attention in positive ways, and honoring all that is sacred. Meditation has many benefits, including a reduction in stress, anxiety, and depression for regular practitioners. Other wonderful benefits are increasing peaceful energies, clarifying your perception, and improving your overall well-being.

You don't need to wait for any particular moon phase to perform this meditation. However, noting whether the moon is waxing, waning, full, or new will help you weave the current lunar energy into your intentions with this mediation. A waxing moon represents rising energy, a waning moon releases energy, a full moon is powerful and key for manifestation, and a new moon is perfect for quiet reflection and new ideas.

The meditation below recommends a pre-meditation bath or shower to assist with offloading old, stagnant energies from the mundane world. This mediation also pairs well with the Mabon Cleansing spell on page 111 to cleanse away stagnant energies from a space.

You can adapt the meditation below to fit any practice or intention. Below, you'll find an optional ingredient for an offering. It's always good practice to prepare something for the deity you look to connect with in exchange for their wisdom and time. This could be a floral arrangement, baked goods, or other meaningful items you've made.

You will need:

- White candle
- Matches
- Optional: Offering for deity

Preparation:

1. Cleanse away old or stagnant energies from your being with a shower or bath, focusing on your intentions. It's best to begin the meditation with a clean slate.

2. Prepare your altar or meditation space with optional decorations, images, statues, or crystals. Set the white candle in front of you. Feel free to make the altar as elaborate or simple as you'd like.

The Meditation:

1. Cast a circle if you feel called to by calling upon the elements.

2. Sit in a comfortable position and light your candle.

3. Mentally prepare for your meditation in silence by focusing only on your breath.

4. Allow your breath to carry you deeper into a relaxed state, and to let all of your worries drift away.

5. Now, imagine yourself walking down a path away from where you're sitting, outside, moving closer to a forest, free from civilization. You notice the sounds of the wind, wrapping around you. The crunch of the leaves on the ground, and the soft sounds of nature moving through the meadow. Your breath is now in sync with nature.

6. Once deep into the forest, you find yourself on the edge of an open meadow filled with an abundance of flowers. The meadow calls you to the center of the Triple Goddess's sanctuary.

7. Immediately upon entering the center, you're surrounded by the presence of the Triple Goddess. Feel the energy all around you, wrapping you in acceptance and loving guidance.

8. Focus on your question, intentions, or problems where guidance is needed. Ask the Triple Goddess for wisdom and listen closely to her words of wisdom. Allow yourself to be open and receptive to her message.

9. Now, having heard the Triple Goddess's wisdom, give your thanks as you make your way back along the same path you took to find her sanctuary. Allow the feelings of calm, love, and guidance envelop your being as you gradually return back towards civilization.

10. You see your altar coming into view. Sit in the same position you left and begin to focus on wiggling your toes and fingers. Slowly awaken back into the present.

11. Blow out your candle and thank the Triple Goddess for her presence.

12. (Optional) Leave an offering for the Triple Goddess overnight.

13. If you've cast a circle, it's now time to open it and release the elements.

14. Reflect on the messages you've received tonight and allow yourself to feel at ease.   *– Ambrosia Hawthorn*

28 Monday

Moon ○ in Gemini ♊
Moon ○ v/c 10:01 pm

29 Tuesday

Moon ○ enters Cancer ♋ 5:28 am
Full Moon ○ 10:28 pm

Long Nights Moon

30 Wednesday

Moon ○ in Cancer ♋

31 Thursday

Moon ○ in Cancer ♋
Moon ○ v/c 8:45 am
Moon ○ enters Leo ♌ 1:58 pm

1 Friday

Moon ○ in Leo ♌

Platonic love, self confidence, self expression, vacation, leisure time, courage, taking risks, performing in public, childbirth, good cheer, gambling, amusement, creativity, loyalty, fine arts. ★ Self care & me time are important. Courage to move forward and progress with Soluna Eyes and Lips. Be creative, take a leap of faith, bring in the light. Close our the dark, leave behind P, S. and I banish the negativity they bring

Set in Eastern Standard Time (EST)

NEW YEAR'S RESOLUTIONS AND MAGICAL INTENTIONS

Have you ever made a New Year's resolution and kept it forever more? While some people do succeed in the long term with this annual tradition, it seems that failure is a more typical result. Psychologists have offered several explanations for why people give up on their resolutions, such as overly general or unrealistic goals. But perhaps the biggest reason keeping a New Year's resolution is so difficult is that most people – non-magical people, that is – are trying to do it all by themselves.

One core difference between resolutions and magical intentions is that Witches are knowingly harnessing the energies of the Universe to assist them with their goals. There are countless spells for breaking bad habits, banishing addictions, losing weight, and becoming healthier, all of which incorporate assistance from the unseen realms. Magic is about the use of one's will, but that's not the same thing as relying solely on one's willpower to make difficult changes – it can definitely be argued that Witches have the advantage here!

Another important distinction is that Witches choose the timing of their intentions from a magical standpoint, which may take astrological data, the day of the week, and/or other occult correspondences into consideration. January 1, by contrast, is a relatively arbitrary point in time to initiate change (though it does have numerological significance).

Whatever your magical intentions are for this year, know that you can begin at any point along the Wheel that works best for you. You have the willing support of the Universe to manifest your desires, so have fun creating inspired magic that helps you succeed!

– *Lisa Chamberlain*

---

2 Saturday *Whilst focusing on self care and*
Moon ☽ in Leo ♌ *the courage to move forward, as the*
Moon ☽ v/c 5:00 pm *Moon enters Virgo, I will continue*
Moon ☽ enters Virgo ♍ 8:13 pm *to work on my health, diet*
and how these help me to heal form P.S. I
hope to put my business into practice and
this will enable me to move forward and progress

3 Sunday *Positive thinking for Soluna Eyes &*
Moon ☽ in Virgo ♍ *Lips to do well. Hoping for a*
positive start soon. I'm ready to work hard
and achieve my goals. This will aid
with the cleansing and purification of
the negativity that surrounds me, whilst
I'm at P.S. Invest in me, exercise to move.

January

4 Monday Bit difficult to focus on my

Moon ☽ in Virgo ♍ healing today, going back to
Moon ☽ v/c 4:34 pm work tomorrow. I tried a bit of
health, to deal with the negativity in my
head. Treadmill and exercise take my mind
away from the thoughts and feelings, for a bit.

5 Tuesday Moving into legal matters and justice.

Moon ☽ enters Libra ♎ 12:42 am I'm going to be optimistic
about being able to move on. Thinking about
contracts, beauty, peace and balance,
getting a bit of support from the federation
would enable me to focus on moving on,
being positive and bringing me some harmony.

6 Wednesday Justice, peace and balance ◑
That's things that I want in my
Waning Half Moon ☽ in Libra ♎ 4:37 am life. This is why I
Mars ♂ enters Taurus ♉ 5:27 pm want to move on and
away from the negativity of P.S. Moving
into Taurus, I'm aware that I need to improve
my self esteem, again moving on will help.
Patience will prevail.

7 Thursday Dave told me that Sam has covid,

Moon ☽ in Libra ♎ so I've not to go in until Monday. I
Moon ☽ v/c 12:54 am asked about homeworking and
Moon ☽ enters Scorpio ♏ 3:53 am again its fallen on deaf ears.
No balance, peace of
mind or harmony, as this situation just
creates worry, anxiety and stress for me. I am
trying to show courage and willpower, its hard.

8 Friday Regeneration and renewal. Today

completed my next course. Picked up
Moon ☽ in Scorpio ♏ my CG to work on transforming
Mercury ☿ enters Aquarius ♒ 7:00 am myself, my future and
Venus ♀ enters Capricorn ♑ 10:41 am my M.H. I am continually
Moon ☽ v/c 8:58 pm hoping for positivity and moving
forward. I'm aiming for new career paths, long
term rewards and trying to work on making

others feel good/better. *Set in Eastern Standard Time (EST)*

CHICORY FOR GROUNDING AND STRENGTH

Chicory is often viewed as a roadside pest, with its vivid purple flowers and rickety stems infiltrating lawns and grassy patches across the globe. But the plant has a history as rich as its flavor, with its use dating back to the Romans for medicinal and culinary purposes. A common green, chicory's leaves are widely used in salads and other leafy meals. Historically, it was also paired with coffee to make small coffee supplies stretch during trade disruptions, as well as to enhance the taste of coffee with its complimentary strong flavor.

Chicory root's hardiness and its robust flavor, as well as its abundance, makes it prime for strength spells, especially those in which confidence and bold courage are needed. Even better, because of its ubiquity, an efficient spell for strength can be a simple, mindful cup of chicory-infused coffee or a quick salad.

To use chicory to its full magickal potential, add one part coffee to a half-part of chicory root and brew to a desired strength. Save the grounds. Pour the strained liquid into a cup and stir in any additives, ensuring that you stir deosil (clockwise). Stir slowly as you meditate on the challenge ahead and, when you feel you've built enough energy, state:

"I meld the grounds and in these circles, a foundation starts to brew:
Strength and courage amid my constraints, a bastion of fortitude."

Plant or scatter the grounds at the northern direction for grounding and strength.

— Sarah Justice

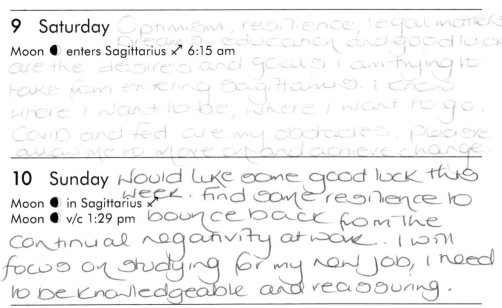

9 Saturday

Moon ● enters Sagittarius ♐ 6:15 am

Optimism, resilience, legal matters, Dreams, education and good luck are the desires and goals I am trying to take from entering Sagittarius. I know where I want to be, where I want to go. Covid and fed are my obstacles, please allow me to move on and achieve change.

10 Sunday

Moon ● in Sagittarius ♐

Moon ● v/c 1:29 pm

Would like some good luck this week. Find some resilience to bounce back from the continual negativity at work. I will focus on studying for my new job, I need to be knowledgeable and reassuring.

11 Monday

Moon ● enters Capricorn ♑ 8:30 am

Heal from depression, i don't seek recognition from work. i would love to focus on my new career path. I do have ambition this is why I would love to progress with my new job. Today was tough, felt like pressure.

12 Tuesday

Moon ● in Capricorn ♑

I felt positive for a little bit yesterday when I had finished my vipers in the afternoon, it was nice to be welcomed back, even if it wasn't from my colleagues. Hopefully I'm one step closer to moving on.

13 Wednesday

New Moon ● in Capricorn ♑ 12:00 am
Moon ● v/c 2:22 am
Moon ● enters Aquarius ♒ 11:44 am

New moon, I lit my first candle tonight and being guided by Wicca orange was my candle of choice. I hope for justice in my legal matters and the opportunity to move on successfully. I welcome in the light.

14 Thursday

Moon ● in Aquarius ♒
Uranus ♅ D 3:36 am
Moon ● v/c 4:28 am

15 Friday

Moon ● enters Pisces ♓ 5:17 pm

NEW MOON MUGWORT DIVINATION TEA

Mugwort is associated with astral travel, divination, psychic visions, and spirit communication, due to its unique chemical properties that induce a mild trance-like state. While this trance is best induced via smoking, a simple mugwort tea is also capable of opening your Third Eye and granting you a heightened ability to communicate with spirits.

Combined with cinnamon, a known energy amplifier, this tea packs a powerful punch if drunk before astral travel, lucid dreaming, tarot or rune readings, or other forms of divination and is best used on the New Moon, but also works well on the Full Moon. Note: Do NOT use mugwort if you are pregnant or wishing to become pregnant.

You will need:

- 1 tsp dried mugwort
- 1 cinnamon stick
- 1 cup hot water
- Sugar or honey to taste

Instructions:

Pour the hot water over the dried mugwort and allow it to steep for 10 minutes. Sweeten to taste, as mugwort is extremely bitter. Stir the tea clockwise using the cinnamon stick while saying,

"Witch's herb, proud and true, unlock my sight on this moon so [new/full]. Grant me visions yet unknown, and open my mind to the visions shown."

Hold the cup in both of your hands and envision it filling with purple light. Finally, drink up and perform your divination ritual of choice.

– Autumn Willow

---

16 Saturday

Moon ◗ in Pisces ♓

---

17 Sunday

Moon ◗ in Pisces ♓
Moon ◗ v/c 10:44 pm

18 Monday

Moon ☽ enters Aries ♈ 2:07 am

19 Tuesday

Moon ☽ in Aries ♈
Sun ☉ enters Aquarius ♒ 3:40 pm

Sun enters Aquarius (Air)

20 Wednesday

Moon ☽ in Aries ♈
Moon ☽ v/c 3:29 am
Moon ☽ enters Taurus ♉ 1:56 pm
Waxing Half Moon ☽ 4:01 pm

21 Thursday

Moon ☽ in Taurus ♉

22 Friday

Moon ☽ in Taurus ♉
Moon ☽ v/c 4:28 pm

POSITIVITY SIGIL SPELL

Sigils are a powerful form of magic. This positivity sigil is a unique creation that can be drawn either on a stone to be carried with you, or carved into a candle to be burned. Use a yellow pencil or marker, for positivity and happiness, to draw your sigil on the piece of paper.

What is truly important with sigils is your intention and the words you'd like to use, as you will see below, as these will literally create the appearance of your sigil.

You will need:

- Stone (I recommend using a river stone, or a rock with a flat surface to turn into a charm) or yellow candle
- Yellow marker or pencil   • Piece of paper
- Permanent marker (if using stone)   • Matches (if using candle)
- Athame or other carving tool (if using candle)

Instructions:

On the sheet of paper, write *"I attract to me, positivity."* Or, write a short phrase of your own. Deconstruct the letters of the phrase into basic shapes, such as curves, dots, dashes, and lines. This is a creative process with no right or wrong approach, so allow your intuition to guide you. Next, combine the basic shapes to form the outline of a shape. This shape is your sigil.

Focus your intentions on the sigil and will it to become active and energized. Re-draw your sigil on the stone, or carve it into the candle. Carry the stone with you, repeating the phrase you used to create the sigil whenever you want to boost its energy. Or, burn the candle when you want to activate your sigil.   *– Severina Sosa*

---

23 Saturday
Moon ☽ enters Gemini ♊ 2:43 am

---

24 Sunday
Moon ☽ in Gemini ♊

---

25 Monday

Moon ○ in Gemini ♊
Moon ○ v/c 2:17 am
Moon ○ enters Cancer ♋ 1:52 pm

26 Tuesday

Moon ○ in Cancer ♋

27 Wednesday

Moon ○ in Cancer ♋
Moon ○ v/c 12:55 pm
Moon ○ enters Leo ♌ 9:54 pm

28 Thursday

Full Moon ○ in Leo ♌ 2:16 pm

Wolf Moon

29 Friday

Moon ○ in Leo ♌
Moon ○ v/c 8:53 pm

DRESSING A CANDLE FOR MAGIC

Candles are a fun and almost fundamental part of magical practice; many witches have all manner of colors and styles of candle at hand ready to weave magic. When it comes to preparing a candle for spell work or ritual, a good way to add extra power and intention is to dress the candle. Dressing a candle can take many forms, but the most basic is to simply anoint it with olive oil and set your intention. However, you can take it one step further and dress it with herbs and oils.

Creating an oil infused with herbs directed toward the magical purpose you have in mind adds an extra boost to your candle magic. Work the oil from the center in both directions, making sure you coat the candle evenly but not thickly. If you wish to be more specific, anoint the candle toward you in order to draw something to you, or away from you in order to banish something.

Powdered herbs are best for dressing a candle, as herbal bits can catch alight, causing a fire hazard. Powdered herbs also stick better to the candle base. Simply anoint the candle with your oil of choice and roll the candle in the herbal blend until the candle is reasonably covered.

With jar candles or seven-day candles, poke three to five holes in the top, drip some oil in each hole, and sprinkle the herbs over the same holes. This adds intention into the large candle and helps contain the magic in one space while burning.

– Stacey Carroll

---

30   Saturday

Moon ○ enters Virgo ♍ 3:02 am
Mercury ☿ ℞ 10:51 am

Mercury retrograde until February 20

---

31   Sunday

Moon ○ in Virgo ♍

February

1 Monday

Moon ☽ in Virgo ♍
Moon ☽ v/c 6:10 am
Moon ☽ enters Libra ♎ 6:25 am
Venus ♀ enters Aquarius ♒ 9:05 am

2 Tuesday

Moon ☽ in Libra ♎

Imbolc

3 Wednesday

Moon ☽ in Libra ♎
Moon ☽ v/c 1:15 am
Moon ☽ enters Scorpio ♏ 9:14 am

Imbolc cross-quarter day 9:40 am

4 Thursday

Waning Half Moon ☽ in Scorpio ♏ 12:37 pm

5 Friday

Moon ☽ in Scorpio ♏
Moon ☽ v/c 4:20 am
Moon ☽ enters Sagittarius ♐ 12:16 pm

Set in Eastern Standard Time (EST)

A QUIET AND COZY IMBOLC

For many, Imbolc arrives at one of the dreariest points in the year. February often feels like a cold, final stretch towards springtime. Yet even though winter still has its hold at Imbolc, it is a time of hope. There is an energetic shift taking place – a feeling of inspiration stirring as spring slowly approaches. Imbolc may not be as wild, animated, or even as popular as Beltane or Samhain, but it is still a wonderful holiday for witches, with many magical opportunities. Here are some simple activities to turn into traditions for a cozy Imbolc.

- **Meditate** – even a few minutes of focusing on deep breathing can bring your attention to the present moment. Use the time to contemplate what you wish to bring into your life.
- **Light candles and use your fireplace** – give yourself a comfortable feeling surrounded by the warm glow of candles and a crackling fire.
- **Take a purifying and relaxing bath** – draw a bath and add a couple drops frankincense, sandalwood, and lavender along with two cups of epsom salt.
- **Prepare for early Spring gardens** – If you garden, Imbolc is a great time to start planning. Begin to plot out when you can start seedlings and creating beds for the earliest growing plants.
- **Magical writing** – Imbolc is a wonderful time to write down plans, goals, and magic. Consider using the time to work in your Book of Shadows or even writing poetry in honor of the goddess Brigid.
- **Eat a comforting meal** – Imbolc is traditionally the time when animals began to lactate, making it a holiday associated with dairy. So, indulge in some cheesecake, hot white chocolate, or fondue for Imbolc!

– Kiki Dombrowski

6   Saturday

Moon ◑ in Sagittarius ♐

7   Sunday

Moon ◑ in Sagittarius ♐
Moon ◑ v/c 1:16 am
Moon ◑ enters Capricorn ♑ 3:52 pm

8 Monday

Moon ● in Capricorn ♑

9 Tuesday

Moon ● in Capricorn ♑
Moon ● v/c 12:22 pm
Moon ● enters Aquarius ♒ 8:20 pm

10 Wednesday

Moon ● in Aquarius ♒

11 Thursday

●

New Moon ● in Aquarius ♒ 2:06 pm
Moon ● v/c 2:06 pm

12 Friday

Moon ● enters Pisces ♓ 2:23 am

ENCHANTING IVY

Also known as: English ivy, Ceridwen
Sacred to: Arianrod, Attis, Bacchus/Dionysus, Cernunnos, Mabon, Ogma
Name in Ogham: *Gort* or *Oir*
Magickal Aspects and Uses: divination, luck, fidelity, love, boundaries & protection
*Poisonous, use with caution

Gort is the twelfth letter of the Ogham alphabet. Its name means "green field" or "garden." "Ceridwen" is a compact evergreen ivy variety with 3-lobed leaves displaying shades of green and yellow. This species makes a good houseplant and is named in honor of the Goddess Cerridwen. In ancient forest gardens, the growth of ivy was encouraged and revered. There is evidence that people created forest openings to help English ivy grow because it was a favorite food of red deer. Ivy patches like these served as feeding grounds encouraging deer to graze, which allowed people to hunt deer more successfully in the winter. This practice also reflects ivy's association with Cernunnos, the Celtic Horned God of nature, fertility, and the forest.

Use ivy in spells related to communication and harmonious connections in communities, group matters, and relationships. Ivy is strongest when it is used with other plants as it demonstrates the lesson of connectivity. Ivy is sacred to the Goddess Arianrod and can be used to commune with her essence and wisdom. In preparation for connecting with this goddess, create a circle of ivy marking the boundary of where you will practice, then invite Arianrod in to work with you. If you don't have the space or ability to create a large circle, you can make a wreath of ivy for the same purpose.

— Leandra Witchwood

13 Saturday

Moon ◗ in Pisces ♓

14 Sunday

Moon ◗ in Pisces ♓
Moon ◗ v/c 2:28 am
Moon ◗ enters Aries ♈ 10:54 am

February

15 Monday

Moon ◐ in Aries ♈

16 Tuesday

Moon ◐ in Aries ♈
Moon ◐ v/c 7:16 pm
Moon ◐ enters Taurus ♉ 10:11 pm

17 Wednesday

Moon ◐ in Taurus ♉

18 Thursday

Moon ◐ in Taurus ♉
Sun ☉ enters Pisces ♓ 5:44 am

Sun enters Pisces (Water)

19 Friday

Moon ◐ in Taurus ♉
Moon ◐ v/c 2:28 am
Moon ◐ enters Gemini ♊ 11:03 am
Waxing Half Moon ◐ 1:47 pm

Set in Eastern Standard Time (EST)

MONEY CHARM SPELL

Charms are effective bundles of magic that can be carried to attract or protect. They are a great way to craft objects imbued with intentions, and can be made with just about any cloth, fabric, or even jars. A charm can also be used to power poppets with properties and correspondences.

The items in this charm contain correspondences to attract money. You can substitute any of the ingredients below with other items that also have money correspondences. Herbs you can substitute are cinnamon, basil, or marigold. Other stones that would work well are pyrite, tiger's eye, aventurine, or amber. To craft a money charm for a loved one or friend, add something that belongs to them.

You will need:

- 1 tbsp dried mint leaves
- 6 inch piece of fabric
- String
- 1 coin
- Citrine stone

Instructions:

1. Cleanse your altar and ingredients.
2. Lay out the square piece of fabric.
3. One by one, imbue each item with your intention and place it on the cloth.
4. Once all items are on your cloth, bundle up the sides and close with the string.
5. Hold the finished charm in your hands and say:

   "With this charm, I draw to me: money, luck, and prosperity."

6. Your charm bag is charged and ready to be carried.
7. Repeat the incantation while holding the charm often.

– Ambrosia Hawthorn

20 Saturday

Moon ☽ in Gemini ♊
Mercury ☿ D 7:52 pm

Mercury direct

21 Sunday

Moon ☽ in Gemini ♊
Moon ☽ v/c 1:39 pm
Moon ☽ enters Cancer ♋ 10:53 pm

22 Monday

Moon ◑ in Cancer ♋

23 Tuesday

Moon ◑ in Cancer ♋
Moon ◑ v/c 11:54 pm

24 Wednesday

Moon ◑ enters Leo ♌ 7:23 am

25 Thursday

Moon ○ in Leo ♌
Venus ♀ enters Pisces ♓ 8:11 am

26 Friday

Moon ○ in Leo ♌
Moon ○ v/c 6:32 am
Moon ○ enters Virgo ♍ 12:07 pm

CHARM FOR PROTECTION

Protection is a very important element in witchcraft. With the work we do and the realms we traverse, it is always a good idea to have spiritual protection over us at all times. It can be elaborate or as simple as you like; oftentimes a small charm bag for protection is all you need.

You will need:

- A handful of one or more protective herbs: rue, bay, rosemary, agrimony, angelica, burdock, calamus, dragon's blood, elder, fennel, garlic, horehound, hyssop, lavender, marshmallow, mint, nettle, pennyroyal, plantain, sage, St. John's wort, valerian, vervain, and/or witch hazel
- Two or more protective stones such as: obsidian, black tourmaline, onyx, jet, and/or smokey quartz
- Small drawstring bag that can hold herbs
- Protection oil
- Protective talisman (such as the Hamsa or Third Pentacle of Jupiter)

Instructions:

Gather your herbs, gemstones and talismans together and place in your charm bag, charging each individual ingredient as you add it in. Hold the charm bag in your hands and visualize a seal of protection around it. Take the oil and anoint the bag in a five fold pattern (each corner and one in the center). Run the bag through some incense smoke to purify and charge it. When you have done that recite the following:

"By the power of my will this charm is charged.
By these breaths I give it life. (Breathe into it three times.) By this smoke
I feed the spirit within (run it through the incense smoke.) I thank you, Spirit of
the Charm, for your protection and strength. As I Will It, So It Is."

– Stacey Carroll

27 Saturday

Full Moon ○ in Virgo ♍ 3:17 am

Snow Moon

28 Sunday

Moon ○ in Virgo ♍
Moon ○ v/c 10:58 am
Moon ○ enters Libra ♎ 2:17 pm

March

1 Monday

Moon ○ in Libra ♎

2 Tuesday

Moon ○ in Libra ♎
Moon ○ v/c 9:09 am
Moon ○ enters Scorpio ♏ 3:38 pm

3 Wednesday

Moon ○ in Scorpio ♏
Mars ♂ enters Gemini ♊ 10:29 pm

4 Thursday

Moon ◐ in Scorpio ♏
Moon ◐ v/c 11:09 am
Moon ◐ enters Sagittarius ♐ 5:43 pm

5 Friday

Waning Half Moon ◐ in Sagittarius ♐ 8:30 pm

Set in Eastern Standard Time (EST)

SEED FERTILITY SPELL BOTTLE

Spring is a time of new life and new beginnings as seeds sprout, baby animals are born, and the Earth begins to warm under the heat of the Sun. As such, this is the perfect time for fertility magic. This spell, which is best performed during the waxing moon, uses seeds to promote fertility, rose quartz for love, and mint for growth – all sealed in a spell bottle to concentrate the energy. It can be used to promote pregnancy, or a successful garden.

You will need:

- Small bottle with cork
- Rose quartz chips
- Candle wax (preferably green, the color of fertility)
- Seeds
- Dried mint

Instructions:

Begin by cleansing your spell ingredients by blowing on them, as this not only removes unwanted energy, but also infuses the objects with your essence. Next, place the seeds in the bottle while saying,

"With these seeds I plant my intentions for the future.
Just as they contain new life, so shall [I/my garden]."

Next, add the rose quartz while saying,

"May these chips of rose quartz bring love, compassion,
and youth so that life may be born in love."

Finally, add the mint while saying,

"Mint, rapid and quick, hasten this spell to bring me the new life I seek.
Just as you grow wild and free so shall the life within [me/my garden]."

Place the cork in the spell bottle and seal with the candle wax. Place the spell jar under your bed or carry it on your person to encourage pregnancy, or bury in your garden to promote a fruitful bounty.   **– Autumn Willow**

---

6   Saturday

Moon ☽ in Sagittarius ♐
Moon ☽ v/c 4:44 am
Moon ☽ enters Capricorn ♑ 9:20 pm

---

7   Sunday

Moon ☽ in Capricorn ♑

---

8 Monday

Moon ☽ in Capricorn ♑
Moon ☽ v/c 7:52 pm

9 Tuesday

Moon ☽ enters Aquarius ♒ 2:41 am

10 Wednesday

Moon ☽ in Aquarius ♒
Moon ☽ v/c 10:32 pm

11 Thursday

Moon ☽ enters Pisces ♓ 9:44 am

12 Friday

Moon ☽ in Pisces ♓

RABBIT MAGICK

Rabbits are an ancient symbol for magick and the unknown. The rabbit connects us to the otherworld, the place where spirits and alternate realities lurk. What exists in the otherworld depends on belief, but the rabbit can guide us to connection with the otherworld, to speak to spirits, commune with deities, or simply to see an alternative perspective.

Begin a meditative session by finding a comfortable place. Enter a trance state by rocking your upper torso in a slow, repetitive movement and humming. Envision yourself amid fog, which disperses until you can see yourself sitting in a grassy clearing surrounded by woods. A rustling in the hedge ahead captures your attention, and you spot a small black rabbit nibbling on wild parsley. The rabbit pauses and looks in your direction. You follow the rabbit. Take in all that the five senses are experiencing in this meditation to truly place yourself there.

You venture near the rabbit and it turns its back to you. It hops a little forward to an entrance into the wood. Tall grasses frame the entrance like a garden gate; the rabbit hops across the threshold and you follow.

What emerges for you in your meditation? Who do you find? What do you see? What symbols emerge? This can be your subconscious or your deities speaking to you. No matter what happens, make sure when you are done with your visualization, you follow the black rabbit out of the wood and back to your seated space. He is the guide that ensures your journey is safe and that you find your way back to reality safely.

– Sarah Justice

---

13 Saturday   ●

New Moon ● in Pisces ♓ 5:21 am
Moon ● v/c 11:38 am
Moon ● enters Aries ♈ 6:44 pm

---

14 Sunday

Moon ● in Aries ♈

---

15 Monday

Moon ● in Aries ♈
Mercury ☿ enters Pisces ♓ 6:26 pm
Moon ● v/c 11:40 pm

16 Tuesday

Moon ● enters Taurus ♉ 6:56 am

17 Wednesday

Moon ● in Taurus ♉

18 Thursday

Moon ● in Taurus ♉
Moon ● v/c 4:40 pm
Moon ● enters Gemini ♊ 7:47 pm

19 Friday

Moon ◗ in Gemini ♊

OSTARA, THE SABBAT OF RENEWAL

Ostara is the spring (or "vernal") equinox, a date when day and night are equal in length. This date also marks the halfway point between Yule, the winter solstice, and Litha, the summer solstice. After Ostara, the days begin to grow noticeably longer until Litha, the longest day of the year.

The word "equinox" itself comes from the Latin phrase aequinoctium, which means "equal night." Day and night are equal in length at this time because of the positions of earth's tilt and orbit. This makes Ostara, along with its counterpart at the autumnal equinox, Mabon, an occasion to focus on what we want to balance in our lives.

Many often think Ostara is the spring festival, but it's actually the second spring festival in the Wheel of the Year — Imbolc is the first (even though there's often still a lot of winter frost!). Ostara has associations with the fertility of the land, and is a time for celebrating the evidence of new life growing all around us. Nature has restarted after having slumbered during the winter, making this sabbat a great time to focus on rebirth and renewal.

Take some time to celebrate the new life that surrounds you in nature. Allow yourself to be present with the new foliage emerging from the trees in your neighborhood. If you can, hike through a forest to feel the Earth's growing energy. It's the perfect time to shake off winter's dormancy and plant your intentions for the rest of the year.

— Severina Sosa

---

20 Saturday

Moon ☽ in Gemini ♊
Sun ☉ enters Aries ♈ 5:37 am

Ostara / Spring Equinox 5:37 am

Sun enters Aries (Fire)

---

21 Sunday

Moon ☽ in Gemini ♊
Moon ☽ v/c 8:04 am
Moon ☽ enters Cancer ♋ 8:17 am
Venus ♀ enters Aries ♈ 10:16 am
Waxing Half Moon ☽ 10:40 am

---

22 Monday

Moon ☽ in Cancer ♋

23 Tuesday

Moon ☽ in Cancer ♋
Moon ☽ v/c 11:26 am
Moon ☽ enters Leo ♌ 5:56 pm

24 Wednesday

Moon ☽ in Leo ♌

25 Thursday

Moon ☽ in Leo ♌
Moon ☽ v/c 9:27 am
Moon ☽ enters Virgo ♍ 11:25 pm

26 Friday

Moon ☽ in Virgo ♍

STINGING NETTLE FOR PROTECTION

Also known as: *ortiga ancha*, nettle, *urtica dioica*

Sacred to: Thor

Element: Fire

Magickal Aspects and Uses: Exorcism, cleansing, healing, protection, purification, lust

Nettle tea is excellent for purification, both energetically and physically. Full of vital nutrients, nettle is an effective alterative which helps bring balance back into the body. The healing and balancing powers of nettle are further reflected in magick. Use nettle in healing spells as a tea or tonic, or carry it in a sachet. When you are feeling off, or need to regain balance as you walk your path, drinking nettle tea in meditation can help bring you back to center.

Use nettle to wash your doors, walls, and floors when performing protection spells. Use the leaves as a sacred barrier around your home. Wreaths and bundles of nettle can be hung from your doors for the same purpose.

In Celtic lore, nettle marks the places where the Fae live and could protect a person from sorcery. A related theme is found in an old Nordic folk tale, where a young girl is tasked with returning her twelve brothers back to their human form after they've been turned into swans. To achieve this, she has to knit them coats (or sweaters, in some versions) from nettles which are harvested from a graveyard at night. Furthermore, she must not speak to anyone until all the garments are complete. The act of bringing her brothers back into human form using nettle is symbolic of using our power to overcome adversity and protect the ones we love from harm.

– Leandra Witchwood

27 Saturday

Moon ○ in Virgo ♍
Moon ○ v/c 7:48 pm

28 Sunday

Moon ○ enters Libra ♎ 1:22 am
Full Moon ○ 2:48 pm

Storm Moon

29 Monday

Moon ○ in Libra ♎
Moon ○ v/c 8:08 pm

30 Tuesday

Moon ○ enters Scorpio ♏ 1:33 am

31 Wednesday

Moon ○ in Scorpio ♏
Moon ○ v/c 8:28 pm

1 Thursday

Moon ○ enters Sagittarius ♐ 1:58 am

2 Friday

Moon ○ in Sagittarius ♐

KYANITE FOR SPIRITUAL CONNECTION

Somewhat lesser known in magical circles than other blue stones like lapis lazuli and blue opal, kyanite is a powerful stone in its own right. Named from the Greek kyanos, meaning "deep blue" (though found in other colors as well), this crystal is excellent for strengthening psychic skills and fostering deep meditation. As a primarily blue stone, it is connected to the throat chakra, but also has an affinity with the third eye and astral travel. It assists with raising your vibration, aligning the chakras, grounding, and gaining mental clarity about emotionally charged situations.

Magical uses

Kyanite pieces are usually long, narrow, and somewhat pointed, making them good for wand tips and crystal grids. Our pagan ancestors used kyanite as a kind of pendulum to navigate journeys into unfamiliar territory, suspending it from a string to follow the magnetic force of the Earth. Work with kyanite in magic for communication (whether with the spirit world or other people), balancing masculine and feminine energies, dream recall, and spiritual development. Carry it with you to speaking engagements or when you need to communicate your needs effectively.

Caring for kyanite

Due to its high vibrational frequency, kyanite is said to never need cleansing, as it doesn't pick up negative energy. However, it's still advisable to cleanse any stone when you first acquire it, and there's nothing wrong with continuing to do so. Effective methods for cleansing and charging kyanite include bells or chimes, burying it in the earth, or leaving it moonlight. Don't submerge kyanite in water (though a quick rinse can be okay), or bury it in salt.

– Lisa Chamberlain

3   Saturday

Moon ☾ in Sagittarius ♐
Moon ☾ v/c 1:23 am
Moon ☾ enters Capricorn ♑ 4:13 am
Mercury ☿ enters Aries ♈ 11:41 pm

4   Sunday

Waning Half Moon ☽ in Capricorn ♑ 6:02 am

5 Monday

Moon ☽ in Capricorn ♑
Moon ☽ v/c 3:05 am
Moon ☽ enters Aquarius ♒ 9:03 am

6 Tuesday

Moon ☽ in Aquarius ♒

7 Wednesday

Moon ☽ in Aquarius ♒
Moon ☽ v/c 6:05 am
Moon ☽ enters Pisces ♓ 4:30 pm

8 Thursday

Moon ☽ in Pisces ♓

9 Friday

Moon ☽ in Pisces ♓
Moon ☽ v/c 7:48 pm

MOSS SPELL FOR PROTECTION

There are many different types of moss: beautiful ground-cover moss that acts as a faerie carpet; moss that shoots into the air; elegant, low-hanging Spanish moss that drapes from trees. No matter the type, mosses correspond to protection and grounding. This makes sense; mosses do provide protective qualities to the earth, keeping moisture in the dirt so that plants can thrive. And they offer a literal ground on which life grows. This spell mimics the tradition of hanging fisher floats as talismans to protect one's property.

You will need:

- Glass jar with a lid, ideally one you can hang
- Dirt collected from underneath the moss
- A tablespoon of water
- Moss, hand-gathered. Lift the moss from the ground to snag the roots.
- Twine or another method of hanging the jar

Instructions:

Place dirt into jar and sprinkle in water. Invoke the earth element by stating:

"North, the pillar of fertility and strength
Of grounding the center and renewing my faith, I invoke you."

As you add the moss, state:

"I call on the mosses to protect my soul, My lovers and kin, my travels,
my home, It roots down and stretches, a veritable shield, An earthy rendition
of a sword that one wields, The home is the bastion, its safety unmatched, Our
beings are safeguards when we're unattached, Only the agreeable
may open this shield, And all negativity is heretofore sealed."

Hang the jar outside the home or place on the ground along the northern side of the property. As the moss grows, so too will the strength of the spell. Add water to the jar periodically to encourage growth.   **– Sarah Justice**

10 Saturday

Moon ● enters Aries Y 2:11 am

11 Sunday   ●

New Moon ● in Aries Y 10:31 pm

12 Monday

Moon ● in Aries Y
Moon ● v/c 8:06 am
Moon ● enters Taurus ♉ 1:44 pm

13 Tuesday

Moon ● in Taurus ♉

14 Wednesday

Moon ◑ in Taurus ♉
Venus ♀ enters Taurus ♉ 2:22 pm
Moon ◑ v/c 8:00 pm

15 Thursday

Moon ◑ enters Gemini ♊ 2:35 am

16 Friday

Moon ◑ in Gemini ♊

BALANCING BERGAMOT BALM

Bergamot is an energizing scent that also is wonderful for relaxing. It's an especially nice oil to use during mundane or stressful days. Bergamot essential oil also pairs well with lemongrass or lavender if you have them on hand. Its base scent is citrus. You can also get creative if you have unscented lotions, or creams that you'd like to infuse with Bergamot's properties. With all essential oils, it's important to perform a patch test on your inner elbow to make sure you don't have any reaction to the mix. Generally speaking, a 2% dilution works well. That equates to 3 drops per 1 tbsp of carrier oil. This makes it safe to use on most skin types who aren't prone to allergies.

You will need:
- 1 tbsp olive oil or other carrier oil
- 6 drops bergamot essential oil
- Amber roller bottle or dropper bottle

Instructions:
1. Cleanse your items.
2. Pour carrier oil into roller or dropper bottle.
3. Add in the bergamot essential oil and chant:

"Mix and blend, my bergamot friend,
Balance and imbue through and through."

4. Hold the bottle in your hands and envision energy wrapping around it. Charge it with your intentions.
5. Shake before using on your forehead or pressure points.

– Ambrosia Hawthorn

---

17 Saturday

Moon ☽ in Gemini ♊
Moon ☽ v/c 11:03 am
Moon ☽ enters Cancer ♋ 3:25 pm

---

18 Sunday

Moon ☽ in Cancer ♋

---

19 Monday

Moon ◐ in Cancer ♋
Mercury ☿ enters Taurus ♉ 6:29 am
Sun ☉ enters Taurus ♉ 4:33 pm
Moon ◐ v/c 8:03 pm

Sun enters Taurus (Earth)

20 Tuesday

Moon ◐ enters Leo ♌ 2:10 am
Waxing Half Moon ◐ 2:59 am

21 Wednesday

Moon ◑ in Leo ♌

22 Thursday

Moon ◑ in Leo ♌
Moon ◑ v/c 8:05 am
Moon ◑ enters Virgo ♍ 9:08 am

23 Friday

Moon ◑ in Virgo ♍
Mars ♂ enters Cancer ♋ 7:49 am

SEEING FAERIES SALVE

This herbal salve is great for working with faeries. Remember that the Fae are Otherworldly beings, historically known for their mischief and supernatural abilities. Working with them requires knowledge, respect, and the intention for the relationship to be mutually beneficial.

First, gather your dried herbs:

- 2 teaspoons each: rose, lavender
- 1 teaspoon each: chamomile, mugwort, calendula, thyme, yarrow, vervain
- 1 teaspoon dried flower petals from your garden or nearby wooded areas. (Check for toxicity first.)

Instructions:

1. Put ½ cup coconut oil in a saucepan and warm up over low heat – do not let it get hot or the herbs will burn. Add the herbs and steep for thirty minutes, stirring occasionally.
2. Pour the oil through a mesh strainer into a Pyrex measuring cup, pressing the herbs gently to get most oil out.
3. Pour the oil mix into a bowl on a double boiler. Add 1 tablespoon each of beeswax and sweet almond oil. Stir until completely melted and blended.
4. Remove from heat and let cool for a few minutes. Stir in 7 drops each of jasmine and rose oil, 1 drop each of rosemary and lemongrass oil, and 1 drop honey.
5. Pour blend into a small tin or glass container. Top with a four-leafed clover, if you have one, or with fluorite, malachite, and/or moonstone chips.

Apply the salve to your pulse points when deepening your connection to the Fae through magic, meditation, and study. Keep it on your altar or wherever you leave offerings to the Fae. Do not rub on your eyes, and be especially mindful if you have allergies or sensitive skin.   *– Kiki Dombrowski*

---

24 Saturday

Moon ○ in Virgo ♍
Moon ○ v/c 6:50 am
Moon ○ enters Libra ♎ 12:06 pm

---

25 Sunday

Moon ○ in Libra ♎

---

26 Monday

Moon ○ in Libra ♎
Moon ○ v/c 8:39 am
Moon ○ enters Scorpio ♏ 12:18 pm
Full Moon ○ 11:31 pm

Pink Moon

27 Tuesday

Moon ○ in Scorpio ♏
Pluto ♇ R 4:02 pm

28 Wednesday

Moon ○ in Scorpio ♏
Moon ○ v/c 8:31 am
Moon ○ enters Sagittarius ♐ 11:42 am

29 Thursday

Moon ○ in Sagittarius ♐

30 Friday

Moon ○ in Sagittarius ♐
Moon ○ v/c 9:26 am
Moon ○ enters Capricorn ♑ 12:16 pm

BELTANE SYMBOLISM

Beltane is an ancient Celtic festival celebrated throughout the United Kingdom and Ireland on the first of May. It traditionally celebrated the peak time of fertility and growth, the halfway point between spring and summer, when everything was lush, growing and coming into its own.

Beltane is a fire festival, and during this time bonfires would be lit in celebration. Farmers brought their livestock to the bonfire to have them cleansed and purified before putting them to pasture for the coming summer. Couples would dance, feast, and be merry while enjoying the freedom of each other's company. Many a baby could be traced back to May Day! New couples would come together to be handfast: committing to one another for a year and a day before deciding if they wished to continue on in marriage or go their separate ways. Couples would sometimes jump the broomstick, signifying leaving one life for another, crossing the threshold from the old to the new.

The symbols of Beltane are vibrant and life affirming: rich ripe strawberries, honey with its gorgeous liquid amber color, cream, salads of leafy greens corresponding to the greenery abounding in the fields and forests, wine made from elderflower, linden and other wildflowers, and mead. The cauldron – the womb of creation, the rabbit – a strong symbol of fertility, hawthorn wood or blossoms – a token of the Fae, and bright spring wildflowers – all of these can adorn an altar to celebrate Beltane. Take joy in the warmth of Spring, in the renewal of life around you, and know that the spirit of the Goddess and the Green Man walk with you during this time.

– Stacey Carroll

---

1 Saturday

Moon ☽ in Capricorn ♑

Beltane

---

2 Sunday

Moon ☽ in Capricorn ♑
Moon ☽ v/c 10:38 am
Moon ☽ enters Aquarius ♒ 3:31 pm

May

3 Monday

Waning Half Moon ☾ in Aquarius ≈ 3:50 pm
Mercury ☿ enters Gemini ♊ 10:49 pm

4 Tuesday

Moon ☾ in Aquarius ≈
Moon ☾ v/c 8:05 pm
Moon ☾ enters Pisces ♓ 10:08 pm

5 Wednesday

Moon ☾ in Pisces ♓

Beltane cross-quarter day 2:36 am

6 Thursday

Moon ☾ in Pisces ♓

7 Friday

Moon ☾ in Pisces ♓
Moon ☾ v/c 3:36 am
Moon ☾ enters Aries ♈ 7:52 am

Set in Eastern Daylight Time (EDT)

BEETROOT FOR SPELLS

Beetroot is one of a kitchen witch's most versatile tools. Its strong flavor makes its powder ideal in drinks, and its vivid purple-red hue is helpful in color magick, producing enchanted inks and tinting the color of tonics and oxymels. In its powdered form, beetroot is also perfect for creating incense, be it loose or hand-formed into cones. For sabbats, it's an ideal root vegetable for Samhain celebrations, where we focus on our ancestral roots and honor the collective "witch" consciousness, as well as the last harvest.

Beetroot corresponds to inner and outer beauty, as well as love and sex, which also makes it ideal for Beltane and Ostara, and its common appearance in grocery stores means we don't have to wait until harvest to get it.

Simply boil the beetroot until a fork glides smoothly into it and eat your magick, or add a ½ teaspoon of beetroot powder into a fruity tea or smoothie (the taste is rather strong, so add in small amounts and continue to taste). Or, sprinkle the powder in with loose resin to create incense. No matter how you use it, try repeating the following beauty charm as you work:

"I call upon Maiden to encourage lust
A passion sits deep in the veins and the bust
I call upon Mother for courage and acceptance
To speak of myself with the most respectful discretions
I call upon Crone for her wisdom and strength.
To know that I'm divine with an unyielding faith.
I ask Mother Earth for sustenance and health
For an outer presence to match this renewed inner wealth."

– Sarah Justice

8   Saturday

Moon ◗ in Aries ♈
Venus ♀ enters Gemini ♊ 10:01 pm

9   Sunday

Moon ● in Aries ♈
Moon ● v/c 6:50 pm
Moon ● enters Taurus ♉ 7:46 pm

May

10 Monday

Moon ● in Taurus ♉

11 Tuesday

●

New Moon ● in Taurus ♉ 3:00 pm

12 Wednesday

Moon ● in Taurus ♉
Moon ● v/c 8:23 am
Moon ● enters Gemini ♊ 8:43 am

13 Thursday

Moon ● in Gemini ♊
Jupiter ♃ enters Pisces ♓ 6:36 pm

14 Friday

Moon ◖ in Gemini ♊
Moon ◖ v/c 6:51 am
Moon ◖ enters Cancer ♋ 9:30 pm

Set in Eastern Daylight Time (EDT)

FRIENDSHIP POPPET

Infuse intentions for friendship into a magical poppet. Poppets are a form of representational magic, traditionally used to represent beings during spells and rituals. In this spell, you'll be creating a poppet that contains all of your desired friendship qualities. My favorite poppet material is felt, but any cloth may be used.

You will need:

- 2 fabric squares
- Pencil
- Paper
- Scissors
- Needle and thread
- Polyfill or cotton balls, for stuffing

Instructions:

1. Cleanse your altar and the tools you'll be using.
2. Sketch a doll-shaped outline onto one of the pieces of fabric. (The less detailed your outline is, the easier it will be to make the poppet).
3. Stack the pieces of fabric to cut. Cut slightly outside your lines so there's extra room to sew the edges.
4. Thread your needle and sew the pieces together. Leave about an inch free so you can turn your poppet inside out.
5. On a piece of paper, write down a list of qualities you'd like a friend to have.
6. Fold or roll the piece of paper and place it inside of your poppet.
7. Fill the rest of the poppet with polyfill or cotton.
8. Seal the poppet.
9. While holding it, focus on your intentions to attract a friend with the qualities you've chosen.
10. Leave the poppet on your altar.   *– Ambrosia Hawthorn*

15 Saturday

Moon ◑ in Cancer ♋

16 Sunday

Moon ◑ in Cancer ♋

17 Monday

Moon ☽ in Cancer ♋
Moon ☽ v/c 2:22 am
Moon ☽ enters Leo ♌ 8:44 am

18 Tuesday

Moon ☽ in Leo ♌

19 Wednesday

Waxing Half Moon ☽ in Leo ♌ 3:12 pm
Moon ☽ v/c 3:12 pm
Moon ☽ enters Virgo ♍ 4:59 pm

20 Thursday

Moon ☽ in Virgo ♍
Sun ☉ enters Gemini ♊ 3:37 pm

Sun enters Gemini (Air)

21 Friday

Moon ☽ in Virgo ♍
Moon ☽ v/c 3:56 pm
Moon ☽ enters Libra ♎ 9:35 pm

BACKYARD WEEDS FOR MAGIC

One of the wonderful things about the plant world is that it is accessible to everyone: you can discover that there is magic in the plants and flowers found right in your backyard. There are many guides to herbal magic that can help you identify the plants growing all around you. You may be surprised by the magical attributes of what so many people consider "weeds."

Broadleaf plantain can be used in healing and empowering magic, offering you energy when you are feeling tired or comfort when you are feeling uneasy. The lovely yellow buttercups that dot many lawns also have an old folk magic use: farmers would rub the flowers on their cows' udders to ensure rich and plentiful dairy production. You can use buttercups to draw prosperity – gather buttercups, chamomile, and dill and place the bouquet in a vase. Keep it on your altar and light a green candle to draw money to you.

Chickweed is a common "weed" that is edible and nutritious. It can also be an ingredient in love and friendship spells. Clovers are used for protection, luck, healing, and love spells. White clover blossoms will protect you from negativity, while red clover can be used for love and beauty magic. Carry clover leaves for good luck and use clover in faery magic. Dandelion is used for enhancing psychic wisdom and supporting divination work. Ground ivy can be used to conjure energies of love, blessings, and joy. Beautiful purple violets can be used in love and friendship spells. They bring a feeling of love and beauty to a home when brought indoors.

– Kiki Dombrowski

---

22 Saturday

Moon ☽ in Libra ♎

---

23 Sunday

Moon ☽ in Libra ♎
Saturn ♄ R 5:19 am
Moon ☽ v/c 5:36 pm
Moon ☽ enters Scorpio ♏ 11:00 pm

---

24 Monday

Moon ☽ in Scorpio ♏

25 Tuesday

Moon ☽ in Scorpio ♏
Moon ☽ v/c 5:19 pm
Moon ☽ enters Sagittarius ♐ 10:39 pm

26 Wednesday

Full Moon ○ in Sagittarius ♐ 7:14 am

Flower Moon

Lunar Eclipse 7:14 am – 5° Sag♐ 26'

27 Thursday

Moon ○ in Sagittarius ♐
Moon ○ v/c 1:35 pm
Moon ○ enters Capricorn ♑ 10:23 pm

28 Friday

Moon ☾ in Capricorn ♑

CRYSTAL RELATIONSHIP "FORECAST"

Getting to know a new love interest is exciting, but can also be stressful. It's easy to get caught up trying to analyze everything about them. But obsessive thinking prevents you from seeing things clearly, creating confusion and doubt. This spell can help you get a sense of your romantic prospect's true potential. You may get a definitive yes or no, or receive information or insight that helps you come to a conclusion on your own. Or, you may be guided to simply stay open and unattached to outcomes for now.

Ideal stones for this spell include amethyst (helps to dispel illusions and keep "obsessive thinking" in check), malachite (particularly appropriate if your current concern stems primarily from a prior relationship experience), and quartz (a good all-purpose intuition booster and helps clear out inner turmoil).

You will need:

- 1 small amethyst, malachite, or quartz crystal
- Small strip of paper

Instructions:

Spend some time getting grounded and centered. Write the person's name on the paper, and ask for any and all illusions you may have about the person to be cleared away. You may want to say the following (or similar) words:

> "Universe, please light the path that I am meant to see,
> with regard to [name of person] and me."

Fold the paper and place it on your altar, underneath the crystal. When you go to bed, place both items under your pillow. You may receive further information in your dreams, or new information of some kind will come to you in your waking life within the next 48 hours.   — *Lisa Chamberlain*

---

29 Saturday

Moon ○ in Capricorn ♑
Moon ○ v/c 6:15 pm
Mercury ☿ ℞ 6:34 pm

Mercury retrograde until June 22

---

30 Sunday

Moon ○ enters Aquarius ♒ 12:04 am

---

31 Monday

Moon ◐ in Aquarius ♒

1 Tuesday

Moon ◐ in Aquarius ♒
Moon ◐ v/c 2:13 am
Moon ◐ enters Pisces ♓ 5:07 am

2 Wednesday

◐

Waning Half Moon ◐ in Pisces ♓ 3:24 am
Venus ♀ enters Cancer ♋ 9:18 am

3 Thursday

Moon ◐ in Pisces ♓
Moon ◐ v/c 7:10 am
Moon ◐ enters Aries ♈ 1:58 pm

4 Friday

Moon ◐ in Aries ♈

HERBAL JAR FOR PSYCHIC WORK

A jar is a great tool for adding different elements together to bring about a specific purpose, and the finished product promotes a daily focus on your goal. Jars have a long history in witchcraft and folk magic, and have been used for protection (think witches bottles that are found under doors, in walls, or buried), sweetening relationships (as in honey jars), and other purposes. This herbal jar for psychic work serves as a talisman, or point of focus, for your divination practice.

Your psychic herbal jar can sit within your sacred space where you work divination, lending some serious spiritual energy when you want to connect with the other realms. Simply gather your herbs together and place them in your container of choice. You can also add different elements, such as gemstones or charms, to give an additional boost.

Some herbs that work beautifully for psychic work are: rose petals, jasmine flower, mugwort, spearmint, cinquefoil, calendula, dandelion, meadowsweet, chamomile, marjoram, vervain, and cinnamon.

Empower Your Jar

Gather your herbs together and place in the jar. Close your eyes and breathe deeply. Focus your energy into the herbal blend. Hold the jar within your hands and say the following:

"Psychic sight, eyes wide open. I seek to see what is to come,
I seek to see what has been before. Open my third eye and allow me to see.
Bring clarity of vision and knowledge, and the wisdom to understand.
As I Will It, So Shall It Be"

— Stacey Carroll

---

5   Saturday

Moon ◖ in Aries Y
Moon ◖ v/c 6:47 pm

---

6   Sunday

Moon ◖ enters Taurus ♉ 1:46 am

June

7 Monday

Moon ☽ in Taurus ♉

8 Tuesday

Moon ☽ in Taurus ♉
Moon ☽ v/c 11:07 am
Moon ☽ enters Gemini ♊ 2:47 pm

9 Wednesday

Moon ☽ in Gemini ♊

10 Thursday

●

New Moon ☽ in Gemini ♊ 6:52 am
Moon ☽ v/c 1:37 pm

Solar Eclipse 6:52 am – 19° Gem♊ 47'

11 Friday

Moon ☽ enters Cancer ♋ 3:22 am
Mars ♂ enters Leo ♌ 9:34 am

Set in Eastern Daylight Time (EDT)

LAVENDER SWEET DREAMS TEA SPELL

Lavender is a calming and relaxing herb that promotes peaceful dreams, happiness, and healing. You can also use this spelled tea for meditation, and lavender's psychic properties make it a good one to sip before divination practices.

Lavender has a fairly intense, tangy taste, so you may want to add a sweetener, such as honey. You can also add other herbs that would complement lavender – such as lemon balm, chamomile, or mugwort.

You will need:

- Kettle
- 1 teaspoon dried lavender
- Mug (use a favorite mug, or one dedicated to the purpose of magical teas)
- Tea ball strainer (or empty tea bag)
- Water

Instructions:

Place the kettle on to boil, and place the dried lavender in the tea ball strainer or tea bag. When the water reaches boiling, take the kettle off the heat and let sit for 30 seconds to one minute, to avoid scorching the herbs. When the water has cooled a bit, place the tea ball of lavender in your mug and pour over with boiled water.

Steep the tea, covered, for 10 minutes. During that time recite the incantation to raise energy:

"Calming lavender, steep and brew,
bestow your powerful energy into me through and through."

Remove the tea ball and mix in any sweetener if desired. Breathe in the aroma of the lavender, focusing on relaxing energy while you wait to enjoy it. When the tea cool enough to drink, visualize the relaxing energy swirling around you until you feel calm and relaxed. — *Severina Sosa*

12 Saturday

Moon ● in Cancer ♋

13 Sunday

Moon ● in Cancer ♋
Moon ● v/c 7:16 am
Moon ● enters Leo ♌ 2:22 pm

14 Monday

Moon ◗ in Leo ♌

15 Tuesday

Moon ◗ in Leo ♌
Moon ◗ v/c 1:27 pm
Moon ◗ enters Virgo ♍ 11:02 pm

16 Wednesday

Moon ◑ in Virgo ♍

17 Thursday

Waxing Half Moon ◑ in Virgo ♍ 11:54 pm
Moon ◑ v/c 11:54 pm

18 Friday

Moon ◑ enters Libra ♎ 4:53 am

FLOWER BOUQUET OIL FOR SELF-LOVE

While self-love cannot be instantly realized with a snap of the fingers or a spell, we can use our magical abilities and the energies of the world around us to help facilitate a space for healing, self-love, and self-awareness. This oil blend combines the aromatherapeutic qualities and magical energies of oils and crystals to assist you in centering yourself, opening your heart chakra, and welcoming love and beneficial opportunities into your life.

In a 4-dram or half-ounce bottle, add the following essential oils:

- 5 drops sweet marjoram
- 5 drops lavender
- 3 drops rose
- 1 drops ylang ylang
- 5 drops jasmine
- 4 drops bergamot
- 3 drops geranium

Instructions:

Fill the bottle halfway with carrier oil. To make this your own energetically unique bouquet, add a couple of drops of up to three of the following optional oils: gardenia, heliotrope, violet, lilac, frangipani, orchid, or carnation. You can also add very small crystal chips to the blend. The best crystals for self-love include rose quartz for gentle love, rhodochrosite for compassion and positive feelings, unakite for healing the heart chakra, rhodonite for self-love and self-forgiveness, and kunzite for loving emotions and positive self-talk.

Fill the bottle to the top with the rest of the carrier oil, close it, and hold it in your hands as you say the following:

"Self-love grows in my heart as I heal,
compassion and tenderness are emotions I feel.
Love surrounds me, love fills me, I understand love and share fully."

– Kiki Dombrowski

---

19 Saturday

Moon ☽ in Libra ♎

---

20 Sunday ☼

Moon ☽ in Libra ♎
Moon ☽ v/c 6:52 am
Moon ☽ enters Scorpio ♏ 7:58 am
Jupiter ♃ ℞ 11:05 am
Sun ☉ enters Cancer ♋ 11:32 pm

Litha / Summer Solstice 11:32 pm

Sun enters Cancer (Water)

June

21 Monday

Moon ☽ in Scorpio ♏

22 Tuesday

Moon ☽ in Scorpio ♏
Moon ☽ v/c 2:43 am
Moon ☽ enters Sagittarius ♐ 8:55 am
Mercury ☿ D 6:00 pm

Mercury direct

23 Wednesday

Moon ☽ in Sagittarius ♐
Moon ☽ v/c 10:09 pm

24 Thursday

Moon ☽ enters Capricorn ♑ 9:05 am
Full Moon ○ 2:40 pm

Strawberry Moon

25 Friday

Moon ○ in Capricorn P
Neptune ♆ R 3:21 pm

Set in Eastern Daylight Time (EDT)

LITHA AND THE SUNSHINE BLUES

With its warm energies and themes of abundance, love, magic, and the peak power of the Sun, Litha is a favorite Sabbat for many. The long days and short nights feel luxurious in comparison to the scant sunlight at Yule. But believe it or not, this time of year isn't everyone's cup of tea, even within the Witching world. Some people struggle with feelings of unease, anxiety, or even depression around the Summer Solstice. These issues may be due to disrupted circadian rhythms caused by increased daylight, which results in decreased melatonin production.

If you find yourself with the sunshine blues, Litha can actually be an opportunity for healing and realigning with the Sun's energy. Here are a few suggestions:

- **Watch the sunset.** Whether in quiet solitude or with merry friends, make a point of observing the end of the longest day of the year. Appreciate the relief you feel as night begins.

- **Light a candle and reflect on the Earth's ever-shifting patterns of light and dark.** From this moment on, we move back toward an equal balance that often means improved sleep for many of us.

- **Work magic for harmonizing with the divine masculine.** Sensitivity to sunlight can be an invitation to address imbalances with the masculine aspects of yourself.

- **Be kind to yourself.** We live in a culture that exalts the summertime, but it's really okay if you don't find it as delightful as autumn or winter. And as the light patterns begin to shift again, you'll still have at least two months to get outside and enjoy the season as you see fit.

— Lisa Chamberlain

26 Saturday

Moon ○ in Capricorn ♑
Moon ○ v/c 8:49 am
Moon ○ enters Aquarius ♒ 10:08 am

27 Sunday

Moon ○ in Aquarius ♒
Venus ♀ enters Leo ♌ 12:27 am
Moon ○ v/c 3:07 pm

28 Monday

Moon ☽ enters Pisces ♓ 1:51 pm

29 Tuesday

Moon ☽ in Pisces ♓

30 Wednesday

Moon ☽ in Pisces ♓
Moon ☽ v/c 1:39 pm
Moon ☽ enters Aries ♈ 9:21 pm

1 Thursday

Waning Half Moon ☽ in Aries ♈ 5:10 pm

2 Friday

Moon ☽ in Aries ♈

Set in Eastern Daylight Time (EDT)

MAGICAL PROPERTIES OF PEACOCK ORE

Peacock ore, also known as bornite, comes in a stunning array of blues, purples, and golds all in one crystal – hence its common name associated with the peacock. While peacock ore is magnificent to behold, it's also a powerful healing crystal. When worn, it will protect you against negative energy and can be incorporated into spells that dispel or ward off negativity, making it perfect for home blessing. Peacock ore can also remove blockages, dispel doubt, and align your energies.

Due to its ability to dispel negativity, peacock ore is known as "the crystal of happiness." With its brilliant rainbow array, it is able to brighten your spirits, even in the darkest of times. It is said that peacock ore can regulate the flow of adrenaline, effectively reducing stress and our flight-or-fight response. Place it somewhere visible to bring calming, happy energies to your home.

Finally, peacock ore is great for astral travel and spirit communication. Since it is naturally calming, it can be used to calm your mind before astral travel or meditation. A calm mind is also a more intuitive mind; thus, peacock ore is great for psychic readings.

You can hold the crystal during these rituals to increase your intuition perception. Combined with its ability to protect the user, this stone is perfect for any work involving spirits.

No matter how you decide to use peacock ore, it is a beautiful addition to any witch's crystal collection!

– Autumn Willow

3 Saturday

Moon ☽ in Aries ♈
Moon ☽ v/c 12:15 am
Moon ☽ enters Taurus ♉ 8:28 am

4 Sunday

Moon ☽ in Taurus ♉

---

5 Monday

Moon ◑ in Taurus ♉
Moon ◑ v/c 12:57 pm
Moon ◑ enters Gemini ♊ 9:24 pm

6 Tuesday

Moon ◑ in Gemini ♊

7 Wednesday

Moon ◑ in Gemini ♊

8 Thursday

Moon ● in Gemini ♊
Moon ● v/c 12:20 am
Moon ● enters Cancer ♋ 9:51 am

9 Friday

New Moon ● in Cancer ♋ 9:16 pm

RELAXING WITH ROSE WATER

Rose is by far one of the most famous flowers in the known world. In the language of flowers, different colors had different meanings, and while this language is largely a forgotten art form, roses have endured as the bud of choice to show others how we feel: red roses for love, yellow for friendship, white for new beginnings, peach for sympathy, and so on.

A lesser-known virtue of the rose plant is the little pods that develop called rosehips – a mighty medicinal punch-packing piece of flora with wonderful benefits. Using rose petals and rosehips together can be highly therapeutic, relaxing, and reviving.

You will need:

- Distilled water
- Rose petals (fresh or dried)
- Rosehips (fresh or dried)
- Rose hydrosol (optional)
- Spray bottle (dark glass is best)

Instructions:

Place the rose petals and rosehips in a saucepan, cover them with hot water, and simmer them gently until the rose petals have lost their color (rosehip will give the water a deep rosy color). Allow the brew to sit covered until it cools completely. Then strain the mixture through cheesecloth or a strainer and funnel the liquid into the bottle.

Now you can get creative. Add rose hydrosol for an added rose punch, and/or witch hazel toner to turn your rose water into a gentle, yet effective facial toner. The rose water can be used in spellwork pertaining to love. If you have a lover coming over, or arguments have happened between yourself and your significant other, enchant your rose spray and mist your home to encourage relaxed, loving, peaceful feelings.   *– Stacey Carroll*

10 Saturday

Moon ● in Cancer ♋
Moon ● v/c 12:10 pm
Moon ● enters Leo ♌ 8:20 pm

11 Sunday

Moon ● in Leo ♌
Mercury ☿ enters Cancer ♋ 4:35 pm

12 Monday

Moon ◐ in Leo ♌
Moon ◐ v/c 8:29 am

13 Tuesday

Moon ◐ enters Virgo ♍ 4:30 am

14 Wednesday

Moon ◐ in Virgo ♍

15 Thursday

Moon ◐ in Virgo ♍
Moon ◐ v/c 2:46 am
Moon ◐ enters Libra ♎ 10:31 am

16 Friday

Moon ◐ in Libra ♎

SOOTHING BASIL

Also known as: Sweet basil, witches herb, American dittany, St. Joseph's wort
Sacred to: Ares, Krishna, Mars, Vishnu and Erzulie
Element: Fire
Magickal Aspects and Uses: Relationships, money, prosperity, wealth, luck, love, exorcism, flying, protection

Basil is well known for its aspects related to wealth and money. It is not always given credit for its ability to soothe tempers and promote the welfare of a business. Place a spring of basil in a spell sachet and keep it in your pocket or wear it around your neck to promote easy transactions and to keep tempers low. If you work in a retail setting, place a live basil plant on the counter near the register. This will help soothe any upset customers, attract new customers, and promote the growth of your business. Basil brings wealth and prosperity to anyone who carries it in their pocket. To help stimulate personal prosperity, place a basil leaf in your wallet to encourage a positive cash flow into your life. You can also rub your bank statement and any form of payment with basil to do the same.

Basil will bring luck to your home as well as soothe tempers triggered by difficult people. Place basil in a centerpiece in your home when you are expecting relatives who are known for arguments or sour dispositions. You may also sprinkle basil on the thresholds of your doorways to prevent evil from entering your home.

— Leandra Witchwood

17 Saturday

Waxing Half Moon ☽ in Libra ♎ 6:10 am
Moon ☽ v/c 7:03 am
Moon ☽ enters Scorpio ♏ 2:38 pm

18 Sunday

Moon ☽ in Scorpio ♏

July

19 Monday

Moon ☽ in Scorpio ♏
Moon ☽ v/c 12:30 pm
Moon ☽ enters Sagittarius ♐ 5:08 pm

20 Tuesday

Moon ☽ in Sagittarius ♐

21 Wednesday

Moon ☽ in Sagittarius ♐
Moon ☽ v/c 6:25 pm
Moon ☽ enters Capricorn ♑ 6:36 pm
Venus ♀ enters Virgo ♍ 8:37 pm

22 Thursday

Moon ☽ in Capricorn ♑
Sun ☉ enters Leo ♌ 10:26 am

Sun enters Leo (Fire)

23 Friday

Moon ☽ in Capricorn ♑
Moon ☽ v/c 12:34 pm
Moon ☽ enters Aquarius ♒ 8:12 pm
Full Moon ○ 10:37 pm

Thunder Moon

Set in Eastern Daylight Time (EDT)

WATER SCRYING

Scrying is a divination practice that reveals images through reflective or shifting surfaces, such as water, flames, mirrors, or crystals. Using water for scrying is often referred to as hydromancy. If you're new to scrying, you may need to practice concentrating your focus on a single spot with a soft gaze. Some may find it helpful to use a wand or athame to gently disturb the surface of the water and look for images in the resulting ripples. A journal isn't strictly necessary, but is useful for recording your impressions.

You will need:

- Dark-colored bowl
- Journal
- Optional: Wand or athame
- Water
- Pen

Instructions:

1. Cleanse your altar and tools.
2. Fill the bowl with water and get in a comfortable position.
3. Focus on your breathing and descend into a meditative state.
4. Center your focus on the water. Look for patterns, images, or symbols. Listen for words, too, and note any other sensory details that pop out at you.
5. If you are struggling to get any impressions, focus on a particular question or intention. You can also try gently creating ripples with your wand or athame.
6. Write down everything that comes to you in a journal for later interpretation.
7. End the session when you become restless.

– Ambrosia Hawthorn

---

24 Saturday

Moon ○ in Aquarius ≈

---

25 Sunday

Moon ○ in Aquarius ≈
Moon ○ v/c 7:13 pm
Moon ○ enters Pisces ♓ 11:30 pm

---

26 Monday

Moon ○ in Pisces ♓

27 Tuesday

Moon ○ in Pisces ♓
Mercury ☿ enters Leo ♌ 9:11 pm
Moon ○ v/c 9:13 pm

28 Wednesday

Moon ◑ enters Aries ♈ 5:57 am
Jupiter ♃ enters Aquarius ♒ 8:42 am

29 Thursday

Moon ◑ in Aries ♈
Mars ♂ enters Virgo ♍ 4:32 pm

30 Friday

Moon ◑ in Aries ♈
Moon ◑ v/c 3:38 pm
Moon ◑ enters Taurus ♉ 4:08 pm

LAMMAS SUN SPELL

At Lammas, we do more than just honor the first harvest. We're honoring the sun for what it lends us before it begins to honor its ancient deal and allow the days to shorten. We can also ask the sun for continued abundance and success.

First, cast a circle and call on the sun at dawn, stating:

"The moon's asleep; Father Sun, arise!
Hearken, now, the day's alive. I've come to you as day opens its eyes,
to harness the knowledge that renders you wise."

If you're in need of goal manifestation or abundance, state the following:

"I ask for abundance, for golden success. A venture that begins from a
foundation at rest. I sowed the seeds with good intention. Prosperity earned
has a long-held retention. I conjure the wisdom and confidence of sun.
I banish concerns until the challenge is won. Success is made manifest
through bergamot rays, of the sun and his power, who coddles the days."

If you want to give thanks, state the following:

"Father, the sun god, the keeper of warmth, the giver of light
when all is forlorn. He drifts over mother when the day is just birthing,
follows the path as the Earth keeps on turning. The sun god drifts over us
in the celestial vault, and into the west, he slips and he falls—
an endless cycle from the keeper of days, who steps back to sleep
in the winter malaise. A swift hearty thanks floats
from tongue to above, to honor the emergence of a golden, tough sun."

– Sarah Justice

---

31 Saturday

Waning Half Moon ◑ in Taurus ♉ 9:16 am

---

1 Sunday

Moon ◑ in Taurus ♉

Lammas

2 Monday

Moon ◐ in Taurus ♉
Moon ◐ v/c 3:41 am
Moon ◐ enters Gemini ♊ 4:46 am

3 Tuesday

Moon ◐ in Gemini ♊

4 Wednesday

Moon ◐ in Gemini ♊
Moon ◐ v/c 3:38 pm
Moon ◐ enters Cancer ♋ 5:17 pm

5 Thursday

Moon ● in Cancer ♋

6 Friday

Moon ● in Cancer ♋
Moon ● v/c 6:11 pm

DARK MOON BANISHMENT SPELL

The Dark Moon is often misunderstood, commonly being confused with the New Moon. During the Dark Moon, the Moon is completely dark. Many witches believe that magic should not performed during the Dark Moon, but this is the perfect time for magic that requires darkness, such as banishment spells and shadow work. This spell uses the dark energies of the Dark Moon to banish negativity, fear, and doubts.

You will need:

- Black candle
- Dried rosemary
- Matches or lighter

- Anointing oil
- Knife

Instructions:

During the night of the Dark Moon, cleanse and consecrate your altar and cast a magic circle if you so desire. Visualize what it is you wish to banish and carve your intention into the candle. Make sure you are specific in your intent – otherwise you run the risk of the spell backfiring. Anoint the candle in oil and roll the candle base in the dried rosemary. Rosemary is a potent banishing herb and thus enhances the power of this spell. Light the candle, and chant your intention aloud at least eight times as the candle burns, visualizing it coming to fruition. Allow the candle to burn out and safely throw away any remains far away from your home.

Note: If you cannot allow the candle to burn all the way down, you can section the candle by carving a divide and writing your intention above it. Only anoint and burn to the section you are working with, leaving the rest of the candle untouched for future use.   *– Autumn Willow*

---

7   Saturday

Moon ● enters Leo ♌ 3:31 am

Lammas cross-quarter day 2:53 am

---

8   Sunday

New Moon ● in Leo ♌ 9:50 am

---

9   Monday

Moon ● in Leo ♌
Moon ● v/c 8:22 am
Moon ● enters Virgo ♍ 10:55 am

10   Tuesday

Moon ● in Virgo ♍

11   Wednesday

Moon ● in Virgo ♍
Moon ● v/c 7:21 am
Moon ● enters Libra ♎ 4:08 pm
Mercury ☿ enters Virgo ♍ 5:57 pm

12   Thursday

Moon ◑ in Libra ♎

13   Friday

Moon ◑ in Libra ♎
Moon ◑ v/c 4:38 pm
Moon ◑ enters Scorpio ♏ 8:01 pm

MAGICKAL BLACKBERRY

Also known as: bramble, cloudberry, goutberry
Sacred to: Brigid and Dagda
Name in Ogham: *Muin*
Magickal Aspects and Uses: communication, grounding, healing, prosperity, protection, purification, connecting with spirits, wealth

A member of the rose family, blackberry is a highly valued, sacred herb of the Celts. Its Celtic name, *Muin*, is likely to have three meanings or associations, one being "cunning," the second being "love" or "esteem," and the third being "deception." (The Celts seemed to have an affinity for trinities.) Blackberry is also associated with the "path of the voice" and is linked to prophetic speech and connecting with the Otherworld and Faeries.

The thorns of the blackberry are curved and sharp, making this plant highly effective in protection magick. Some believe that when you walk by a blackberry vine with sharp thorns, negative energy is cleansed from the body as it is caught by the thorns and pulled away. Grow blackberry near the entrances or on the perimeter of your home to protect your property from unwanted visitors and energies. You may also grow blackberries into an arch, creating a magickal doorway that also acts as a magickal barrier to your sacred space. When the vines are new and before they begin to bear fruit, you can walk through this doorway to infuse your intentions and rituals with renewing springtime energy. As the vines bear fruit, walk through it to infuse yourself with prosperous energy. In the fall, you can use this doorway to help settle your energy as you work toward connecting with the fae, spirits, and other energies often concealed by the veil.

– Leandra Witchwood

14 Saturday

Moon ☽ in Scorpio ♏

15 Sunday

Waxing Half Moon ☽ in Scorpio ♏ 11:19 am
Moon ☽ v/c 11:05 pm
Moon ☽ enters Sagittarius ♐ 11:11 pm

16 Monday

Moon ☽ in Sagittarius ♐
Venus ♀ enters Libra ♎ 12:26 am

17 Tuesday

Moon ☽ in Sagittarius ♐
Moon ☽ v/c 9:43 pm

18 Wednesday

Moon ☽ enters Capricorn ♑ 1:58 am

19 Thursday

Moon ☽ in Capricorn ♑
Moon ☽ v/c 7:59 pm
Uranus ♅ R 9:40 pm

20 Friday

Moon ☽ enters Aquarius ♒ 4:49 am

THE MAGICAL BLUE MOON

The origins of the term "Blue Moon" are thought to come from a few different possible sources, beginning with references going back to the 16th century. Today, the term refers to a Full Moon occurring at an irregular time – an "extra" Full Moon of sorts.

Unlike the relatively recent concept of the calendrical Blue Moon – or the second Full Moon in a calendar month – the more traditional Blue Moon is the third Full Moon in a season in which four Full Moons occur. These seasonal Blue Moons occur roughly every 2 to 3 years. Since there are three Full Moons between Litha and Mabon in 2021, the Full Moon of August 22nd is a Blue Moon.

This tradition comes from farmer's almanacs of the 19th and early 20th centuries, which listed the Full Moons of each year using names borrowed from Native American traditions, many of which are now incorporated into Wiccan and other Pagan practices.

Many Wiccans view the Blue Moon as a time of heightened connection with the Goddess. Spells worked at this time are considered to have even more potency than "ordinary" Full Moon spells. Some even believe that the effects of such magic can have effects lasting until the next Blue Moon!

In particular, magic related to wisdom, love, and protection is effective on these occasions, as are all forms of divination. If you have magical goals that you have previously considered impossible to achieve, this is an excellent time to give it a shot!

— *Lisa Chamberlain*

21 Saturday
Moon ○ in Aquarius ≈

22 Sunday
Full Moon ○ in Aquarius ≈ 8:02 am
Moon ○ v/c 8:02 am
Moon ○ enters Pisces ♓ 8:42 am
Sun ☉ enters Virgo ♍ 5:35 pm

Corn Moon

Blue Moon

Sun enters Virgo (Earth)

23 Monday

Moon ○ in Pisces ♓

24 Tuesday

Moon ○ in Pisces ♓
Moon ○ v/c 5:12 am
Moon ○ enters Aries ♈ 2:57 pm

25 Wednesday

Moon ○ in Aries ♈

26 Thursday

Moon ◑ in Aries ♈
Moon ◑ v/c 5:14 pm

27 Friday

Moon ◑ enters Taurus ♉ 12:26 am

GRASS CORD MAGICK

Many grasses hold spiritual value – especially sweetgrass, affectionately known as "Mother Earth's Hair." Cords are also a means to tie ourselves to the spiritual world, or capture significant moments along our enchanted path. We can combine both spiritual components to connect to Mother Earth to offer thanks and ask for protection. You will need 12-inch lengths of fresh sweetgrass, brown cord, and white cord, along with 10 tiny bells.

Tie the sweetgrass and cords together at one end. Using the white cord, tie a tiny bell above the knot. This ensures that this braided cord begins and stays rooted in good intention.

Begin braiding the cords and grass together downward, with the grass separated as one "cord." After braiding one inch, make a knot by separating the materials into two groups and tying them. Then use the white cord to tie another bell. State: By braid of one, this spell is spun.

Repeat this process, and with each bell and tying of the knot, state the appropriate incantation:

*"By braid of two, they start to root. By braid of three, they start to weave.
By braid of four, the fruits are born. We reach the fifth by bell and braid,
and with insistence the spell is lain. Sixth, to earth this spell we endow;
strength, fortitude, a mindful plow. Seven, the pulse through which
all life's sustained, we embed our thanks, earth manifested as braid.
Eight, we ring to signal the ether, to bless the land that's scarred
and made feeble. By nine, we strengthen our hearty foundation;
to carry us through this year's duration."*

Tie the cords together. Wear or hang the cord.   **– Sarah Justice**

---

28 Saturday

Moon ☾ in Taurus ♉

---

29 Sunday

Moon ☾ in Taurus ♉
Moon ☾ v/c 10:58 am
Moon ☾ enters Gemini ♊ 12:42 pm

---

30 Monday

Mercury ☿ enters Libra ♎ 1:10 am
Waning Half Moon ☽ in Gemini ♊ 3:13 am

31 Tuesday

Moon ☽ in Gemini ♊
Moon ☽ v/c 4:48 pm

1 Wednesday

Moon ☽ enters Cancer ♋ 1:26 am

2 Thursday

Moon ☽ in Cancer ♋

3 Friday

Moon ☽ in Cancer ♋
Moon ☽ v/c 1:37 am
Moon ☽ enters Leo ♌ 11:58 am

Set in Eastern Daylight Time (EDT)

APPLE PROSPERITY SPELL

As Summer ends and Fall begins, a number of fruits and vegetables ripen in the fields. Apples are one of the last fruits of the harvest season, reaching their peak in September and October. This simple spell uses an apple to bring you abundance and prosperity in the coming Winter months, and draws on the symbolic meanings of the rune Fehu (prosperity) and Uruz (perseverance and endurance). You can find images of these runes from the Elder Futhark online. This spell is best performed on a Thursday (the day of wealth) or a Full Moon.

Fehu is the rune of prosperity, while Uruz is the rune of perseverance and endurance.

You will need:

- Apple (any kind)
- Knife
- Cloth (preferably green or gold)

Instructions:

First, wash the apple thoroughly and dry it with the cloth. As you dry the apple, envision it filling with green or golden light – the colors of money and prosperity – while visualizing the results you are seeking.

Next, hold the apple before you and say,

"Apple, sweet and ripe, feed this spell on this night.
Bring me the riches that I seek, so I shall not struggle in the upcoming weeks."

Cut the apple in half, width-wise, to expose the pentacle within the core. Using the knife, carve the Fehu rune on one half and the Uruz rune on the other. Eat the half with the Uruz rune, filling you with the endurance needed to achieve your goals, and bury the Fehu half to feed the spell. As the apple decays, riches will flow continuously to you.   **– Autumn Willow**

---

4 Saturday

Moon ● in Leo ♌

---

5 Sunday

Moon ● in Leo ♌
Moon ● v/c 10:21 am
Moon ● enters Virgo ♍ 7:05 pm

September

6 Monday

New Moon ● in Virgo ♍ 8:52 pm

7 Tuesday

Moon ● in Virgo ♍
Moon ● v/c 3:23 pm
Moon ● enters Libra ♎ 11:20 pm

8 Wednesday

Moon ● in Libra ♎

9 Thursday

Moon ◑ in Libra ♎

10 Friday

Moon ◑ in Libra ♎
Moon ◑ v/c 12:48 am
Moon ◑ enters Scorpio ♏ 2:05 am
Venus ♀ enters Scorpio ♏ 4:39 pm

Set in Eastern Daylight Time (EDT)

HERBAL PILLOW FOR SLEEP

There are some really wonderful herbs to help with relaxation and sleep; some of the more well-known include lavender, chamomile and hops. The best way to ensure a restful, relaxing night's sleep is to put these herbs into a sleep pillow and place it inside of the pillow you sleep on. The scent permeates and fills the senses, triggering the brain to slow down and embrace restfulness. Herbal sleep pillows or sachets are very easy to make, even if you have no sewing skills whatsoever. With so many different fabrics and designs available, customizing your magic has never been so fun!

You will need:

- Two 15cm x 8cm pieces of fabric (or dimensions of your choosing)
- 2 x liner fabric same size (optional)*
- Small amount of stuffing (optional)
- Small handful of one or more herbs: lavender, chamomile, hops, passionflower, linden flower, and/or spearmint

Instructions:

Measure out and cut your fabric. Place the two pieces together with the pattern on the inside, then place the liner (if using) over the top. Stitch about 5mm – 10mm from the edge. Stitch the fourth side about half way, leaving the other half open. Now, turn the pillow inside out so the pattern is on the outside. Place the stuffing (if using) and herbs inside the pillow, and then stitch the opening so the pillow is fully sealed. Enjoy your relaxing herbal pillow!

*The liner is an option if you prefer to have a bit of a buffer between your head and the pillow fabric.

– Stacey Carroll

11 Saturday

Moon ☽ in Scorpio ♏

12 Sunday

Moon ☽ in Scorpio ♏
Moon ☽ v/c 1:33 am
Moon ☽ enters Sagittarius ♐ 4:34 am

13   Monday

Waxing Half Moon ☽ in Sagittarius ♐ 4:39 pm

14   Tuesday

Moon ☽ in Sagittarius ♐
Moon ☽ v/c 6:57 am
Moon ☽ enters Capricorn ♑ 7:34 am
Mars ♂ enters Libra ♎ 8:14 pm

15   Wednesday

Moon ☽ in Capricorn ♑

16   Thursday

Moon ☽ in Capricorn ♑
Moon ☽ v/c 1:40 am
Moon ☽ enters Aquarius ♒ 11:23 am

17   Friday

Moon ☽ in Aquarius ♒

PSYCHIC WORMWOOD

Also known as: Absinthe, absinthium, absinthe wormwood, grand wormwood, old woman

Sacred to: Hecate, Artemis, Diana, Iris

Element: Air and Fire

Magickal Aspects and Uses: Visions, psychic powers, protection, love, calling spirits

*Poisonous, use in small quantities

Wormwood should always be used with care. It is the ingredient in the spirit absinthe, which for a time was banned in certain areas due to its ability to induce hallucinations. Wormwood should only be used in small amounts, as in larger amounts it can be poisonous. It is known for inducing visions and is often used in shadow work, when the unseen must be revealed. Wormwood is traditionally prepared as a tea to be used in flying ointments or tonics.

Wormwood is a very bitter plant and is used to stimulate poor appetites. It is a stomachic herb which helps strengthen and tone the stomach, helping with poor digestive functions of the stomach.

Wormwood is generally good for protection – grow it near your home to help protect it from unwanted evil or negative influences. Burn wormwood before meditation or journey work to help clarify the visions and messages you receive. You can drink tea blended with wormwood to enhance divination, and when calling spirits to your aid. Placing wormwood under the bed is said to draw a loved one near. When driving in dangerous or questionable conditions, hang wormwood from the rear-view mirror to protect your vehicle from danger.
                                                            – Leandra Witchwood

18 Saturday

Moon ◯ in Aquarius ≈
Moon ◯ v/c 5:14 am
Moon ◯ enters Pisces ♓ 4:22 pm

19 Sunday

Moon ◯ in Pisces ♓

20 Monday

Full Moon ○ in Pisces ♓ 7:55 pm
Moon ○ v/c 7:55 pm
Moon ○ enters Aries ♈ 11:13 pm

Harvest Moon

21 Tuesday

Moon ○ in Aries ♈

22 Wednesday

Moon ○ in Aries ♈
Sun ☉ enters Libra ♎ 3:21 pm
Moon ○ v/c 10:05 pm

Mabon / Autumn Equinox 3:21 pm

Sun enters Libra (Air)

23 Thursday

Moon ○ enters Taurus ♉ 8:38 am

24 Friday

Moon ○ in Taurus ♉

Set in Eastern Daylight Time (EDT)

MABON CLEANSING SPELL

Whereas Ostara is about light, rebirth, and fertility, Mabon, at the Autumn Equinox, is about harvesting, death, and the darker aspects of life. Mabon, is often thought of as "the Witch's Thanksgiving," as it is the second harvest festival. As we are preparing to turn inward for the winter months, it's a wonderful time to spruce up the energy of your home.

This cleansing spell features easy-to-source essential oils to clear away clutter and negative energies: lemon for purification and energy attunement, lavender for peace and purification, and cedar for purification and dispelling negativity. Vinegar is an effective natural cleaner for removing dirt and grime.

You will need:

- 20 oz spray bottle
- 8 oz water
- 3 drops lavender essential oil
- 2 tbsp baking soda
- 8 oz distilled vinegar
- 4 drops lemon essential oil
- 2 drops cedar essential oil

Instructions:

1. Cleanse your altar and tools.
2. Add ingredients to the bottle, one at a time, while focusing your intentions.
3. Hold the bottle in your hands and charge for use in purifying and refreshing your home. Spray down your kitchen countertops, windows, and walls, visualizing old, stagnant energies being washed away. Dry with a clean cloth.
4. When the cleaning is complete, speak an incantation:

> "In this kitchen, I banish all that is unwelcome.
> In this home, I purify the energy.
> In this space, I welcome peace and balance."

– Ambrosia Hawthorn

---

25 Saturday

Moon ☽ in Taurus ♉
Moon ☽ v/c 9:09 am
Moon ☽ enters Gemini ♊ 8:36 pm

---

26 Sunday

Moon ☽ in Gemini ♊

---

27 Monday

Moon ☽ in Gemini ♊
Mercury ☿ ℞ 1:10 am

Mercury retrograde until October 18

28 Tuesday

Moon ☽ in Gemini ♊
Moon ☽ v/c 12:18 am
Moon ☽ enters Cancer ♋ 9:34 am
Waning Half Moon ☽ 9:57 pm

29 Wednesday

Moon ☽ in Cancer ♋

30 Thursday

Moon ☽ in Cancer ♋
Moon ☽ v/c 10:48 am
Moon ☽ enters Leo ♌ 8:53 pm

1 Friday

Moon ☽ in Leo ♌

Set in Eastern Daylight Time (EDT)

SALT BALANCE SPELL
TO HONOR SHADOW WORK

Shadow Work involves magic to adjust or honor the not-so-positive qualities of ourselves (like a sharp tongue or bold tenacity), or working through and honoring emotional pain. In shadow work, we accept that these parts hold value and have purpose, even if they aren't always enjoyable. This work is ideal during times of balance – the equinoxes – when the world's own light and darkness achieve a strong, yet malleable, balance.

You will need:

- Coarse sea salt, white
- Black lava salt
- Three smaller bowls (one for each salt)
- Gray salt
- Glass bowl with water in it

Instructions:

Place the bowls of water and salt in front of you. With each of the following lines from the spell, sprinkle a pinch of salt in the water, going from black, to gray, to white, to gray, and then to black again. Repeat the cycle, with the last line dedicated to a last sprinkle of gray, sealing the meld of black and white.

"The embers fight the nightly chill – the kind that comes when life is still.
It sits in the chambers of the heart and the hearth, its battle made manifest
on the grounds of this earth. They strike a cease-fire; an ancient truce,
to acknowledge their facets and their positive use.
A delicate balance of the highest self and the pain that resides
in the deepest of wells. We honor the dark wind, with bright embers upon it
For even honey and vinegar make a strong, stable tonic."

Pour a little of the water at the four cardinal directions of your home until all is poured.

– Sarah Justice

2 Saturday

Moon ☽ in Leo ♌
Moon ☽ v/c 7:43 pm

3 Sunday

Moon ☽ enters Virgo ♍ 4:37 am

October

4 Monday

Moon ● in Virgo ♍

5 Tuesday

Moon ● in Virgo ♍
Moon ● v/c 4:46 am
Moon ● enters Libra ♎ 8:41 am

6 Wednesday   ●

New Moon ● in Libra ♎ 7:05 am
Pluto ♇ D 2:29 pm

7 Thursday

Moon ● in Libra ♎
Moon ● v/c 1:03 am
Venus ♀ enters Sagittarius ♐ 7:21 am
Moon ● enters Scorpio ♏ 10:22 am

8 Friday

Moon ● in Scorpio ♏

Set in Eastern Daylight Time (EDT)

PICTURE JASPER:
GLIMPSES OF AN ANCIENT WORLD

Perhaps one of the most visually stunning mineral stones on the planet, picture jasper (also called "picture stone") may appear humble from a distance in its earthy, opaque shades of brown. Seen up close, however, each stone has a potential world within it – a literal picture, formed by its unique mix of iron and other minerals, along with petrified mud. The bands within this form of jasper show up as pictures, or scenes, when the stone is cut or polished. Often they resemble natural landscapes, but images of objects and even people can also be glimpsed in these miniature masterpieces.

Magical uses

The mesmerizing and often abstract detail of many picture jaspers makes them excellent stones for scrying. You can often use the same stone and see completely different images each time you gaze at it, depending on your question and your frame of mind. Picture jasper is also excellent for ritual and magical work related to Earth energies, as it is literally a visual record of the ancient natural processes happening under the Earth's surface. Use picture jasper in rituals dedicated to the Goddess, and in shamanic journey work related to the distant past.

Caring for picture jasper

As an Earth stone, picture jasper absorbs energy and therefore benefits from regular cleansing. Water and soil are good options, as are sunlight and moonlight, which will also charge the jasper. Keep these beauties in a place where you will see them regularly, and periodically explore their imagery. This will deepen your relationship with your jasper, and increase your receptivity to its messages.   – Lisa Chamberlain

9 Saturday

Moon ◑ in Scorpio ♏
Moon ◑ v/c 2:05 am
Moon ◑ enters Sagittarius ♐ 11:24 am

10 Sunday

Moon ◑ in Sagittarius ♐
Saturn ♄ D 10:17 pm

October

11 Monday

Moon ☽ in Sagittarius ♐
Moon ☽ v/c 12:30 am
Moon ☽ enters Capricorn ♑ 1:15 pm

12 Tuesday

Waxing Half Moon ☽ in Capricorn ♑ 11:25 pm

13 Wednesday

Moon ☽ in Capricorn ♑
Moon ☽ v/c 6:53 am
Moon ☽ enters Aquarius ♒ 4:47 pm

14 Thursday

Moon ☽ in Aquarius ♒

15 Friday

Moon ☽ in Aquarius ♒
Moon ☽ v/c 8:32 am
Moon ☽ enters Pisces ♓ 10:22 pm

Set in Eastern Daylight Time (EDT)

ROSEMARY PROTECTION OIL

Fortify your magical defenses with this protection oil for use in spellwork. Rosemary is known for protection, warding, and banishing negativity. This oil is made by infusing the herb into a carrier oil, such as olive, jojoba, apricot kernel, avocado, sunflower, or almond oil. If you plan on using this oil on your forehead, do a little research on which oil is best for your particular skin type. This oil takes approximately 4–6 weeks to infuse with rosemary's properties. It will remain potent for up to 6–12 months, depending on how you store it.

You will need:

- 2 tsp dried rosemary
- 2 oz olive oil or other carrier oil
- Small strainer and/or cheesecloth
- Funnel

- 2 oz glass jar or bottle
- 2 oz amber glass dropper or roller bottle
- Labeling materials

Instructions:

Set your intentions as you add the rosemary to your jar. Pour the olive oil over the rosemary. As you do this, say the words, *"Rosemary protect, ward, and defend."*

Seal your jar and label with the date. Roll the jar in your hands, focusing on your intentions and repeating the incantation until the oil feels fully charged. Place the jar in a warm, bright place and shake periodically for 4–6 weeks.

When the oil is fully infused, strain the rosemary out and pour the remaining oil into your bottle. To apply, place a dot on your forehead or pressure points, reciting the above incantation. Store the oil in a cool, dark place for maximum shelf life, and discard if it becomes moldy or smells strange. *– Severina Sosa*

---

16 Saturday

Moon ☽ in Pisces ♓

---

17 Sunday

Moon ☽ in Pisces ♓
Moon ☽ v/c 7:24 pm

October

18   Monday

Jupiter ♃ D 1:30 am
Moon ○ enters Aries ♈ 6:04 am
Mercury ☿ D 11:17 am

Mercury direct

19   Tuesday

Moon ○ in Aries ♈

20   Wednesday

Full Moon ○ in Aries ♈ 10:57 am
Moon ○ v/c 10:57 am
Moon ○ enters Taurus ♉ 3:59 pm

Hunter's Moon

21   Thursday

Moon ○ in Taurus ♉

22   Friday

Moon ○ in Taurus ♉
Moon ○ v/c 4:35 pm

Set in Eastern Daylight Time (EDT)

SPELL POUCH TO SEE SPIRITS

This spell pouch combines herbs, crystals, and oils that are associated with spirit communication and psychic abilities. If you make this pouch, please keep in mind that spirit communication is not a light-hearted activity, but one that requires caution and reverence.

You will need a black pouch for this. Gather equal parts of the following herbs to comfortably fit into it along with the crystals:

Lavender – Folklore suggests carrying lavender can help you to see ghosts

Mugwort – To enhance psychic abilities and assist in clairvoyance

Mullein – To see help see spirits, yet protect against harm

Dittany of Crete – An ancient herb connected to clairvoyance and spirit communication

Thyme – To welcome the spirits of nature and the dead

Poplar – Poplar trees are associated with access to the Otherworld. If available in your area, collect three fallen poplar leaves to add to your bag

Combine the herbs in a bowl. Add a piece of howlite, amethyst, and blue lace agate. Add a couple drops of anise and pine essential oils. If you have a small trinket, such as a keepsake from an ancestor or a talisman you use in spiritual work, you can add that as well. Blend the items with your fingers until they are warm to the touch. Place everything into the pouch and tie it shut. Hold the pouch in your hands and say the following incantation:

"With this pouch I can see spirits beyond this place and time. May it protect me from harm, while allowing me to see those that are not of this earthly realm."

Carry the pouch with you whenever you're seeking a supernatural encounter.

– Kiki Dombrowski

---

23 Saturday

Sun ☉ enters Scorpio ♏ 12:51 am
Moon ☽ enters Gemini ♊ 3:57 am

Sun enters Scorpio (Water)

---

24 Sunday

Moon ☽ in Gemini ♊

---

25 Monday

Moon ☾ in Gemini ♊
Moon ☾ v/c 10:11 am
Moon ☾ enters Cancer ♋ 5:00 pm

26 Tuesday

Moon ☾ in Cancer ♋

27 Wednesday

Moon ☾ in Cancer ♋

28 Thursday

Moon ☾ in Cancer ♋
Moon ☾ v/c 2:02 am
Moon ☾ enters Leo ♌ 5:07 am
Waning Half Moon ☾ 4:05 pm

29 Friday

Moon ☽ in Leo ♌

THE SAMHAIN APPLE

Magickal Aspects and Uses: Action, attraction, beauty, divination, fertility, healing, love, luck, peace, power, strength, immortality, and the Divine.

Apples have many uses and associations in magick. The five-pointed star found inside the apple has long been associated with witches, magick, and the power witches can wield. It is also a symbol of the Celtic Cailleach, or crone goddess, and her infinite wisdom. Apple is one of the seven chieftain trees in Irish/Celtic Brehon law and is revered as sacred. This speaks to the intense magickal nature of this fruit and its many virtues.

In the season of Samhain, apples become a particularly prominent symbol. Apples have long been associated with immortality and the presence of the Divine. It is for this reason that apples make an ideal offering to deceased loved ones and ancestors on your Samhain altar. Cut an apple to reveal the five-pointed star and use this symbol as a representation of the "tween," or between, state of Samhain, when the veil between the living and the Otherworld is easily parted.

Make a wand out of apple wood to be used in healing and love spells. Candles can also be made using apple wood for the wick. Apple's association with the Divine makes apple-wood candles especially effective for rituals and meditations where you seek a direct connection with your higher source or pantheon. Placing these handmade candles on your Samhain altar will help ensure that messages from the beyond are delivered and received.

– Leandra Witchwood

---

30 Saturday

Moon ☾ in Leo ♌
Moon ☾ v/c 3:05 am
Mars ♂ enters Scorpio ♏ 10:21 am
Moon ☾ enters Virgo ♍ 2:09 pm

---

31 Sunday

Moon ☾ in Virgo ♍

Samhain

November

1   Monday

Moon ◑ in Virgo ♍
Moon ◑ v/c 1:00 pm
Moon ◑ enters Libra ♎ 7:11 pm

2   Tuesday

Moon ● in Libra ♎

3   Wednesday

Moon ● in Libra ♎
Moon ● v/c 6:32 pm
Moon ● enters Scorpio ♏ 8:52 pm

4   Thursday   ●

New Moon ● in Scorpio ♏ 5:14 pm

5   Friday

Moon ● in Scorpio ♏
Venus ♀ enters Capricorn ♑ 6:44 am
Moon ● v/c 12:10 pm
Mercury ☿ enters Scorpio ♏ 6:35 pm
Moon ● enters Sagittarius ♐ 8:52 pm

AMBER HAPPINESS TALISMAN

Sometimes we all get a little down, but thankfully we can use magic to help ease the blues. This happiness talisman uses amber, which is prehistoric tree sap, to sweeten your mood long-term. Talismans differ from amulets in that they are used to attract a specific benefit to the owner, while amulets are used for protection.

You will need:

• Amber

• Jewelry wire

Instructions:

Cleanse your amber using the cleansing method of your choice, then charge it for at least one hour in sunlight, which will empower it with the energy of the Sun. Sunlight is known to combat depression, and generally we refer to someone who is happy as having a sunny disposition. (To avoid fading or darkening, however, do not leave the amber in direct sunlight for too long.)

After the amber has charged, wrap it in the jewelry wire six times to create a charm (which can also be turned into a key ring!). Six is a solar number and strongly associated with personal responsibility, courage, and security. While creating your talisman charm, chant:

"Bring me happiness, in my time of need.
Banish my blues out to sea. Bring me joy everlasting
and make my sorrows ever fleeting. So I will it, so it shall be."

Carry your newly-created talisman with you or hold it whenever you are feeling down.

– Autumn Willow

---

6 Saturday

Moon ● in Sagittarius ♐

Samhain cross-quarter day 11:50 pm

---

7 Sunday

Moon ◐ in Sagittarius ♐
Moon ◐ v/c 8:44 am
Moon ● enters Capricorn ♑ 8:03 pm

Eastern Standard Time (EST) begins 7 November, 2 am

8 Monday

Moon ◐ in Capricorn ♑

9 Tuesday

Moon ◐ in Capricorn ♑
Moon ◐ v/c 12:51 pm
Moon ◐ enters Aquarius ♒ 10:03 pm

10 Wednesday

Moon ◐ in Aquarius ♒

11 Thursday

◑

Waxing Half Moon ◑ in Aquarius ♒ 7:46 am
Moon ◑ v/c 2:52 pm

12 Friday

Moon ◑ enters Pisces ♓ 2:53 am

YARROW MAGICAL PROPERTIES AND FOLKLORE

One of the flowery queens of the summer months is the meadow and garden-loving yarrow. It could be considered a "magical catch-all" with all of its magical and medicinal uses. Yarrow has long been revered as a healing plant, having been a medical aid on ancient battlefields. In Greek mythology, it is said Achilles used yarrow on wounded soldiers to stop heavy bleeding.

Yarrow has protective powers as well. Scatter the dried herbs on your doorstep to keep away evil influences. Or, create an herbal wand wrapped with yarrow and hang it in your home to keep your space purified and clear of negative energy. There are many old folk charms that use yarrow for love purposes. Place a sprig of yarrow in your pillow to dream about your true love. Use pink yarrow flowers in spells to attract love into your life. Or, carry in a pink pouch with marjoram, rose quartz, and rhodonite while mending a broken heart.

Dried yarrow stalks were used traditionally used to perform the ancient Chinese divination practice of I-Ching. Drink a cup of yarrow and mugwort tea to elevate your psychic senses before performing divination.

Or, leave a small sprig of dried yarrow with your divination tools. Yarrow blossoms in late spring and through the summer – perhaps this is what makes it a flowery favorite of the Fae. Incorporate yarrow into a garden where you wish to attract faeries or leave fresh yarrow blossoms as an offering to them.

– Kiki Dombrowski

13 Saturday

Moon ☽ in Pisces ♓

14 Sunday

Moon ☽ in Pisces ♓
Moon ☽ v/c 12:40 am
Moon ☽ enters Aries ♈ 10:48 am

15 Monday

Moon ◯ in Aries ♈

16 Tuesday

Moon ◯ in Aries ♈
Moon ◯ v/c 10:51 am
Moon ◯ enters Taurus ♉ 9:18 pm

17 Wednesday

Moon ◯ in Taurus ♉

18 Thursday

Moon ◯ in Taurus ♉

19 Friday

Full Moon ◯ in Taurus ♉ 3:57 am
Moon ◯ v/c 3:57 am
Moon ◯ enters Gemini ♊ 9:33 am

Frost Moon

Lunar Eclipse 3:57 am – 27° Tau ♉ 14'

Set in Eastern Standard Time (EST)

HERBAL SALTS FOR CLEANSING

Salt is a very powerful cleanser on its own, but when it's combined with cleansing and purifying herbs and oils, the boost is just fantastic. There are several different ways that herbal salts can be used to cleanse around the home:

Floor sweep – Sprinkle around the home, then focus on sweeping out all negativity and stale energy.

Room deodorizer – Place in a bowl, up high away from pets and children. Empower or bless it to purify and cleanse the home.

On the altar – Use as an offering on your altar to clear the air and provide a spiritually cleansed area.

Spiritual wash – Use on your body to remove negativity from your personal energy field. You can pour it over yourself in the shower, or place it in an organza bag over your shower head, then let the water run through it, cleansing you.

You will need:
- 1 big jar
- 1 cup of Epsom salts
- Essential oils of choice (lemongrass, rosemary, lavender, juniper, clary sage, pine)
- 1 cup of salt of choice
- Cleansing herbs (lemongrass, rosemary, sage, lavender, juniper, hyssop, blessed thistle, bay)

Instructions:
Mix salts, herbs, and oils together in a bowl, saying these (or similar) words over them to empower them for use in cleansing:
> *"Let the air cleanse these herbs, let the energy wash through.*
> *May they strip away any negativity. May they strip away bonds*
> *that no longer serve. Let my spirit be cleansed anew"*

Place the herbal salts in a jar until you are ready to use them.

– Stacey Carroll

20 Saturday

Moon ○ in Gemini ♊

21 Sunday

Moon ○ in Gemini ♊
Moon ○ v/c 10:52 am
Sun ☉ enters Sagittarius ♐ 9:34 pm
Moon ○ enters Cancer ♋ 10:33 pm

Sun enters Sagittarius (Fire)

22 Monday

Moon ☽ in Cancer ♋

23 Tuesday

Moon ☽ in Cancer ♋

24 Wednesday

Moon ☽ in Cancer ♋
Moon ☽ v/c 12:46 am
Mercury ☿ enters Sagittarius ♐ 10:36 am
Moon ☽ enters Leo ♌ 10:58 am

25 Thursday

Moon ☽ in Leo ♌

26 Friday

Moon ☽ in Leo ♌
Moon ☽ v/c 11:23 am
Moon ☽ enters Virgo ♍ 9:12 pm

BANISH ANXIETY CANDLE SPELL

Candle spells are powerful in both attraction and banishing work. This spell uses an infused oil to banish anxiety from the user. Lemon balm is a great herb for calming and reducing anxiety. If you don't have it on hand, however, other herbs and/or essential oils you can use are lavender, basil, chamomile, jasmine, or bergamot. For maximum-strength oil, let the herbs sit in the oil for 3-4 weeks, as this is the optimal herb extraction time. If you don't want to wait for your herbs to infuse, you can use essential oils in lieu of herbs, diluted in a carrier oil.

You will need:

- 1 white candle
- 1 tbsp lemon balm, or 3 drops essential oil
- 1 tbsp olive oil or other carrier oil

Instructions:

1. Cleanse and consecrate your ingredients and tools.
2. Mix together the olive oil and lemon balm while you focus on your intentions to banish anxiety and create space for healing. Set aside for 3-4 weeks to strengthen before continuing, or substitute essential oils instead.
3. Anoint the candle by rubbing the oil blend down the candle with your fingers. Start at the bottom of the candle and work the oil upwards to enhance banishing energy. Do not get oil on the wick.
4. Light the candle and close your eyes.
5. Meditate on your intentions and say:
    "Banish from me, all fear and anxiety."
6. Repeat this incantation as many times as you feel necessary.
7. Visualize all anxiety leaving your being. Repeat this spell whenever you feel the need. You can also use the oil on your pressure points to relieve anxiety.

— Ambrosia Hawthorn

---

27 Saturday

Waning Half Moon ☽ in Virgo ♍ 7:27 am

---

28 Sunday

Moon ☽ in Virgo ♍
Moon ☽ v/c 7:02 pm

---

29 Monday

Moon ☾ enters Libra ♎ 3:55 am

30 Tuesday

Moon ☾ in Libra ♎
Moon ☾ v/c 11:19 pm

1 Wednesday

Moon ☾ enters Scorpio ♏ 6:55 am
Neptune ♆ D 8:22 am

2 Thursday

Moon ● in Scorpio ♏

3 Friday

Moon ● in Scorpio ♏
Moon ● v/c 12:22 am
Moon ● enters Sagittarius ♐ 7:12 am

Sacred to: Cerridwen

Name in Ogham: *Ruis*

Magickal Aspects and Uses: Exorcism, purification, healing, health, protection, prosperity

*Poisonous, except for the ripe berries and flowers

Elder is often tied to the energetic aspects of transformation, regeneration, the cycle of life, death and rebirth, and fate. In many circles, elder is burned to honor the Fae and the Goddess Cerridwen. In some traditions, it is believed that a faerie or the essence of the Goddess lives within the plant. The flowers and ripe berries have many medicinal properties, from helping to reduce fevers to supporting the immune system. The leaves, stems, bark, and roots should be used with caution due to their poisonous properties.

Elder is an excellent plant to use in spells related to closure, protection, and banishing. Plant elder outside your home to help stop and redirect hostile energetic attacks. Elder can also be planted in cemeteries, allowing the dead to rest in peace. Fasten your doors and windows closed with elder to keep the fae and negative energies out of your home. Add the dried crushed leaves to your Samhain incense to help clear negative and stagnant energies. Use the juice and sap to create an anointing mixture. Anoint your third eye with this mixture before performing divination.

Keep in mind that when you work with elder, reverence is important. A proper offering must be made to the spirit of elder. Only after the offering is accepted will your work be successful.

— *Leandra Witchwood*

4 Saturday

New Moon ● in Sagittarius ♐ 2:43 am

Solar Eclipse 2:43 am – 12° Sag♐ 22'

5 Sunday

Moon ● in Sagittarius ♐
Moon ● v/c 12:08 am
Moon ● enters Capricorn ♑ 6:30 am

December

6 Monday

Moon ● in Capricorn ♑
Moon ● v/c 11:42 pm

7 Tuesday

Moon ● enters Aquarius ♒ 6:48 am

8 Wednesday

Moon ◑ in Aquarius ♒

9 Thursday

Moon ◑ in Aquarius ♒
Moon ◑ v/c 4:59 am
Moon ◑ enters Pisces ♓ 9:53 am

10 Friday

Waxing Half Moon ◑ in Pisces ♓ 8:35 pm

Set in Eastern Standard Time (EST)

CITRINE ENERGY BOOST MEDITATION SPELL

Citrine is a stimulating crystal that assists with enhancing the mind. Meditation has the ability to reset the mind, relieve stress, and significantly improve brain function, which results in improved energy. Use this spell whenever you need an energetic lift. You'll feel revitalized, have increased self-awareness, and enjoy a stable, energized state of being. If you do not have access to citrine, you can also do this meditation with a piece of quartz crystal, amethyst, carnelian, or amber, as these stones are also excellent for balancing and boosting energy.

You will need:

• 1 citrine (or other) crystal

Instructions:

Set your intentions as you find yourself a comfortable position. You should have a straight back. However, if you feel seriously depleted and find it difficult to sit up straight, a lying-down position (like the yoga pose Shavasana, or "corpse pose") can be beneficial for you.

Begin by simply focusing on breathing slowly and steadily. Hold the citrine (or other) crystal in your hand and focus your attention and energy on the stone. Once you feel the stone begin to warm, visualize its energy radiating outward.

Focus on the energy and move it to wrap around your entire body. Then, concentrate the energy on where you need it most. This might be your state of mind, or an area of your physical body that has been sluggish. Allow yourself five to ten minutes to hold this energy within until you feel a shift, or a boost in your own energy level. See yourself being further energized with each deep breath.   *– Severina Sosa*

11 Saturday

Moon ☽ in Pisces ♓
Moon ☽ v/c 2:40 pm
Moon ☽ enters Aries ♈ 4:46 pm

12 Sunday

Moon ☽ in Aries ♈

Set in Eastern Standard Time (EST)

December

13 Monday

Moon ☽ in Aries ♈
Mars ♂ enters Sagittarius ♐ 4:53 am
Mercury ☿ enters Capricorn ♑ 12:52 pm
Moon ☽ v/c 9:52 pm

14 Tuesday

Moon ☽ enters Taurus ♉ 3:11 am

15 Wednesday

Moon ☽ in Taurus ♉

16 Thursday

Moon ☽ in Taurus ♉
Moon ☽ v/c 11:08 am
Moon ☽ enters Gemini ♊ 3:42 pm

17 Friday

Moon ☽ in Gemini ♊

APPLE CIDER POTION FOR ABUNDANCE

Apples are an enchanted fruit connected to the Otherworld, ancient goddesses, divination, and mythology. As symbols of beauty, wisdom, fertility, healing, and immortality, apples are used in spells for love, abundance, growth, wellness, pleasure, and magic. For a magical beverage that can conjure abundance, consider brewing this simple and sweet mulled apple cider potion, perfect for a Yule celebration or just a cozy winter's night.

You will need:

- ½ gallon apple cider
- 1 tsp. Cloves, whole
- ¼ tsp. Allspice, powdered
- 2 tbsp. – 4 tbsp. Brown sugar
- 2 tsp. Cinnamon, powdered
- ½ tsp. Nutmeg, powdered
- 3 Orange slices
- 1 tsp. Vanilla extract

Instructions:

1. Pour the apple cider into a large saucepan and warm up over medium heat to bring to a simmer.
2. Add the cinnamon, cloves, nutmeg, allspice, orange, brown sugar, and vanilla extract. Turn down the heat to low.
3. Using a wooden spoon, or your favorite kitchen witch spoon, stir the cider in a clockwise direction. Say the following incantation:
   "May the magic of these apples conjure love and abundance in my life.
   May these spices bring prosperity and wealth into my life.
   May this orange bring brightness and growth to my most valuable endeavors.
   As I drink this, I see abundance manifest in my reality. So mote it be!"
4. Cover the pan and let the cider simmer for 20 to 25 minutes. Serve warm, visualizing the most optimistic outcomes of success and abundance in your projects and goals. — *Kiki Dombrowski*

---

18 Saturday

Full Moon ○ in Gemini ♊ 11:35 pm

Long Nights Moon

---

19 Sunday

Moon ○ in Gemini ♊
Moon ○ v/c 1:02 am
Moon ○ enters Cancer ♋ 4:42 am
Venus ♀ ℞ 5:36 am

December

20 Monday

Moon ○ in Cancer ♋

21 Tuesday

Moon ○ in Cancer ♋
Moon ○ v/c 9:44 am
Sun ☉ enters Capricorn ♑ 10:59 am
Moon ○ enters Leo ♌ 4:53 pm

Yule / Winter Solstice 10:59 am

Sun enters Capricorn (Earth)

22 Wednesday

Moon ○ in Leo ♌

23 Thursday

Moon ◐ in Leo ♌

24 Friday

Moon ◐ in Leo ♌
Moon ◐ v/c 1:39 am
Moon ◐ enters Virgo ♍ 3:24 am

Set in Eastern Standard Time (EST)

YULE POMANDER FOR GOOD LUCK

Pomanders, which originate from the French pomme d'amber ("apple of perfume"), are fruits covered in spices. This traditional Yule gift was popularized during the Middle Ages as a way to protect against pestilence, and thus became associated with recovery, protection, and good luck.

Modern pomanders are usually made of oranges, adorned with whole cloves and cinnamon, and hung with red or gold ribbon. Gift someone a pomander this Yuletide season to bring them good luck and protection in the New Year, or keep it for yourself!

You will need:

- Orange (happiness & health)
- Nail or needle
- Plastic bag
- Red or gold ribbon
- Whole cloves (protection & luck)
- Powdered cinnamon, nutmeg, and ginger to coat (protection & luck)

Instructions:

Begin by setting your intention for your pomander. Hold this intention in your mind as you stick the whole cloves into the orange, using the nail or needle to form the hole for each clove. The cloves will draw closer together as the orange dries out, so be sure to space them apart a bit.

Place the ground herbs in a plastic bag. Add the clove-covered orange and shake to coat.

Allow the orange to sit for two to six weeks to dry out. Once dry, shake off the excess herbs and wrap the orange in the red or gold ribbon, tying a knot around the top and then forming a loop to hang the pomander. Display or give as a gift!

– Autumn Willow

---

25 Saturday

Moon ☾ in Virgo ♍

---

26 Sunday

Moon ☾ in Virgo ♍
Moon ☾ v/c 3:39 am
Moon ☾ enters Libra ♎ 11:24 am
Waning Half Moon ☾ 9:24 pm

December/January

27 Monday

Moon ◖ in Libra ♎

28 Tuesday

Moon ◖ in Libra ♎
Moon ◖ v/c 4:10 pm
Moon ◖ enters Scorpio ♏ 4:16 pm
Jupiter ♃ enters Pisces ♓ 11:09 pm

29 Wednesday

Moon ◖ in Scorpio ♏

30 Thursday

Moon ◖ in Scorpio ♏
Moon ◖ v/c 12:10 pm
Moon ◖ enters Sagittarius ♐ 6:08 pm

31 Friday

Moon ● in Sagittarius ♐

Set in Eastern Standard Time (EST)

RENEWING RITUAL BATH

As the holiday season comes to a close, it's a perfect time to clear out old energy and make way for new, positive developments to come into your life.

You can choose your own combination of crystals, but using at least two types is recommended. Black tourmaline is ideal for releasing heavy burdens or healing from negative experiences. Citrine lends its sunny energies to renewing the body, mind, and spirit after releasing the unwanted. Amethyst promotes balance when beginning anew, while carnelian promotes courage and motivation.

You will need:
- 1 or more clear quartz crystals
- 4 or more pieces black tourmaline, citrine, amethyst, and/or carnelian
- 5–10 drops essential oils: bergamot, cedarwood, geranium, lavender, and/or patchouli (Choose according to your intuition, but use a blend of at least two)
- ½ cup to 1 cup sea salt   • 4 white candles

Instructions:
Place one candle on each corner of the tub, or on a nearby surface. Place the clear quartz in the tub, on the opposite side from the drain, and begin running the bath. Distribute the rest of the crystals evenly on the corners or around the edge of the tub, and pour the salt under the running water. When the tub is nearly full, add the oils.

As you soak, reflect on the sweeter moments of the past year. What blessings did you receive? What would you like to experience more of in the coming year? When you feel ready, unplug the drain and let the water carry away any regrets, dissatisfaction, or other negative feelings you're ready to leave behind. Emerge from the tub renewed and eager for the year to come.

– *Lisa Chamberlain*

1   Saturday

Moon ● in Sagittarius ♐
Moon ● v/c 3:16 am
Moon ● enters Capricorn ♑ 6:02 pm

2   Sunday

Mercury ☿ enters Aquarius ♒ 2:10 am
New Moon ● in Capricorn ♑ 1:33 pm

2021 AT A GLANCE

JANUARY
M	T	W	T	F	S	S
				1	2	3
4	5	6	7	8	9	10
11	12	13	14	15	16	17
18	19	20	21	22	23	24
25	26	27	28	29	30	31

FEBRUARY
M	T	W	T	F	S	S
1	2	3	4	5	6	7
8	9	10	11	12	13	14
15	16	17	18	19	20	21
22	23	24	25	26	27	28

MARCH
M	T	W	T	F	S	S
1	2	3	4	5	6	7
8	9	10	11	12	13	14
15	16	17	18	19	20	21
22	23	24	25	26	27	28
29	30	31				

APRIL
M	T	W	T	F	S	S
			1	2	3	4
5	6	7	8	9	10	11
12	13	14	15	16	17	18
19	20	21	22	23	24	25
26	27	28	29	30		

MAY
M	T	W	T	F	S	S
					1	2
3	4	5	6	7	8	9
10	11	12	13	14	15	16
17	18	19	20	21	22	23
24	25	26	27	28	29	30
31						

JUNE
M	T	W	T	F	S	S
	1	2	3	4	5	6
7	8	9	10	11	12	13
14	15	16	17	18	19	20
21	22	23	24	25	26	27
28	29	30				

JULY
M	T	W	T	F	S	S
			1	2	3	4
5	6	7	8	9	10	11
12	13	14	15	16	17	18
19	20	21	22	23	24	25
26	27	28	29	30	31	

AUGUST
M	T	W	T	F	S	S
						1
2	3	4	5	6	7	8
9	10	11	12	13	14	15
16	17	18	19	20	21	22
23	24	25	26	27	28	29
30	31					

SEPTEMBER
M	T	W	T	F	S	S
		1	2	3	4	5
6	7	8	9	10	11	12
13	14	15	16	17	18	19
20	21	22	23	24	25	26
27	28	29	30			

OCTOBER
M	T	W	T	F	S	S
				1	2	3
4	5	6	7	8	9	10
11	12	13	14	15	16	17
18	19	20	21	22	23	24
25	26	27	28	29	30	31

NOVEMBER
M	T	W	T	F	S	S
1	2	3	4	5	6	7
8	9	10	11	12	13	14
15	16	17	18	19	20	21
22	23	24	25	26	27	28
29	30					

DECEMBER
M	T	W	T	F	S	S
		1	2	3	4	5
6	7	8	9	10	11	12
13	14	15	16	17	18	19
20	21	22	23	24	25	26
27	28	29	30	31		

2022 AT A GLANCE

JANUARY

M	T	W	T	F	S	S
					1	2
3	4	5	6	7	8	9
10	11	12	13	14	15	16
17	18	19	20	21	22	23
24	25	26	27	28	29	30
31						

FEBRUARY

M	T	W	T	F	S	S
	1	2	3	4	5	6
7	8	9	10	11	12	13
14	15	16	17	18	19	20
21	22	23	24	25	26	27
28						

MARCH

M	T	W	T	F	S	S
	1	2	3	4	5	6
7	8	9	10	11	12	13
14	15	16	17	18	19	20
21	22	23	24	25	26	27
28	29	30	31			

APRIL

M	T	W	T	F	S	S
				1	2	3
4	5	6	7	8	9	10
11	12	13	14	15	16	17
18	19	20	21	22	23	24
25	26	27	28	29	30	

MAY

M	T	W	T	F	S	S
						1
2	3	4	5	6	7	8
9	10	11	12	13	14	15
16	17	18	19	20	21	22
23	24	25	26	27	28	29
30	31					

JUNE

M	T	W	T	F	S	S
		1	2	3	4	5
6	7	8	9	10	11	12
13	14	15	16	17	18	19
20	21	22	23	24	25	26
27	28	29	30			

JULY

M	T	W	T	F	S	S
				1	2	3
4	5	6	7	8	9	10
11	12	13	14	15	16	17
18	19	20	21	22	23	24
25	26	27	28	29	30	31

AUGUST

M	T	W	T	F	S	S
1	2	3	4	5	6	7
8	9	10	11	12	13	14
15	16	17	18	19	20	21
22	23	24	25	26	27	28
29	30	31				

SEPTEMBER

M	T	W	T	F	S	S
			1	2	3	4
5	6	7	8	9	10	11
12	13	14	15	16	17	18
19	20	21	22	23	24	25
26	27	28	29	30		

OCTOBER

M	T	W	T	F	S	S
					1	2
3	4	5	6	7	8	9
10	11	12	13	14	15	16
17	18	19	20	21	22	23
24	25	26	27	28	29	30
31						

NOVEMBER

M	T	W	T	F	S	S
	1	2	3	4	5	6
7	8	9	10	11	12	13
14	15	16	17	18	19	20
21	22	23	24	25	26	27
28	29	30				

DECEMBER

M	T	W	T	F	S	S
			1	2	3	4
5	6	7	8	9	10	11
12	13	14	15	16	17	18
19	20	21	22	23	24	25
26	27	28	29	30	31	

ABOUT THE CONTRIBUTORS

Lisa Chamberlain is the successful author of more than twenty books on Wicca, divination, and magical living, including *Wicca Book of Spells, Wicca for Beginners, Runes for Beginners,* and *Magic and the Law of Attraction.* As an intuitive empath, she has been exploring Wicca, magic, and other esoteric traditions since her teenage years. Her spiritual journey has included a traditional solitary Wiccan practice as well as more eclectic studies across a wide range of belief systems. Lisa's focus is on positive magic that promotes self-empowerment for the good of the whole. You can find out more about her and her work at her website, **wiccaliving.com**

Stacey Carroll is a green path hedge witch, certified herbalist, mad gardener, initiated High Priestess, book lover, and divination enthusiast. Her articles have been published in *Witches and Pagans Magazine, The Crooked Path Journal,* and the now-defunct *Australian Pagan Magazine.* A country girl with a bent sense of humor and a passion for her cats, she has been walking the twisted roads of the witch for many a year now. You can usually find her in the garden, with a book in hand, or in the kitchen baking, loving the life of a country witch and herbalist. Her blog, The Country Witch's Cottage, can be found at **www.thecountrywitchscottage.com**

Ambrosia Hawthorn is a traveling eclectic witch and card slinger with indigenous roots in Yup'ik shamanism and Puerto Rican folk magic. She is the owner of the witchcraft blog Wild Goddess Magick, editor of *Witchology Magazine,* and author of *The Spell Book for New Witches* and *Seasons of Wicca.* She found her practice at the age of thirteen and has been studying the craft and her lineage ever since. Ambrosia's goal is to provide material for every kind of witch, and she draws inspiration from the Wheel of the Year to create and share new content about all types of magic.

Leandra Witchwood is the founder of the food and lifestyle blog The Magick Kitchen (**www.TheMagickKitchen.com**), which focuses on Kitchen Witchcraft, herbalism, and interests related to witchcraft, herbs, and magick. She has written a variety of books focused on helping the beginning seeker find their path, such as *Magick in the Kitchen: A Real-World Spiritual Guide for Manifesting the Kitchen Witch Within.* She is also the owner of The Witchwood Teahouse (**www.TheWitchwoodTeahouse.com**), where she offers a variety of organic loose-leaf teas and sacred botanicals for wellness, ceremony, enjoyment, and more. Learn more about Leandra and her work by visiting **LeandraWitchwood.com**

Sarah Justice is the owner of The Tiny Cauldron (**www.tinycauldron.com**), an online cottage filled with ritual items rooted in authentic traditional witchcraft practices. She is also the co-editor of *Witchology Magazine,* and the Salem Magic teacher at Witch With Me's Academy. She loves anything with candlelight and cobblestones, and enjoys sipping coffee and tending to her wildflower daughter, Winnie.

Kiki Dombrowski is a spiritual researcher and explorer who has spent her life studying mythology, magic, witchcraft, and the supernatural. She lives in Savannah, where she is a professional Tarot card reader, certified life coach, and writer. Kiki has worked with various forms of divination, most notably Tarot, which she began working with over 25 years ago. She has published two books – *Eight Extraordinary Days* and *A Curious Future* – both of which are slated for 2nd editions. She has also been a contributing writer for Witch Way Magazine. Kiki received her BA in English and Creative Writing from Southern Connecticut State University. She received her MA in Medieval English from the University of Nottingham. For more information, please visit **kikidombrowski.com** or follow her on Twitter at @KikiD333.

Severina Sosa is an avid writer about witchcraft and a contributor to *Witchology Magazine,* a publication for modern Pagans. She lives near the Yosemite National Park in California with her husband and an abundance of wildlife. Severina is a practiced herbalist, hedge witch, and astrologer. She works with the elements of the natural world, such as the Earth, the sea, weather, and fire magic. Severina is also a psychic who divines with tools such as the Tarot and the stars.

Autumn Willow is a practicing hedge witch of over 15 years and the author behind the blog Flying the Hedge, where she writes about hedge craft, the Wheel of the Year, spirit communication, and folklore. She currently lives in Georgia with her three cats and two chickens, and spends her time teaching high school science, reading, playing World of Warcraft, and remodeling her small home. For more information, visit her website at **flyingthehedge.com**

THREE FREE
AUDIOBOOK PROMOTION

Don't forget, you can now enjoy three audiobooks completely free of charge when you start a free 30-day trial with Audible.

If you're new to the Craft, *Wicca Starter Kit* contains three of Lisa's most popular books for beginning Wiccans. You can download it for free at:

www.wiccaliving.com/free-wiccan-audiobooks

Or, if you're wanting to expand your magical skills, check out *Spellbook Starter Kit*, with three collections of spellwork featuring the powerful energies of candles, colors, crystals, mineral stones, and magical herbs. Download over 150 spells for free at:

www.wiccaliving.com/free-spell-audiobooks

Members receive free audiobooks every month, as well as exclusive discounts. And, if you don't want to continue with Audible, just remember to cancel your membership. You won't be charged a cent, and you'll get to keep your books!

Happy listening!

MORE BOOKS BY
LISA CHAMBERLAIN

Wicca for Beginners: A Guide to Wiccan Beliefs, Rituals, Magic, and Witchcraft

Wicca Book of Spells: A Book of Shadows for Wiccans, Witches, and Other Practitioners of Magic

Wicca Herbal Magic: A Beginner's Guide to Practicing Wiccan Herbal Magic, with Simple Herb Spells

Wicca Book of Herbal Spells: A Book of Shadows for Wiccans, Witches, and Other Practitioners of Herbal Magic

Wicca Candle Magic: A Beginner's Guide to Practicing Wiccan Candle Magic, with Simple Candle Spells

Wicca Book of Candle Spells: A Book of Shadows for Wiccans, Witches, and Other Practitioners of Candle Magic

Wicca Crystal Magic: A Beginner's Guide to Practicing Wiccan Crystal Magic, with Simple Crystal Spells

Wicca Book of Crystal Spells: A Book of Shadows for Wiccans, Witches, and Other Practitioners of Crystal Magic

Tarot for Beginners: A Guide to Psychic Tarot Reading, Real Tarot Card Meanings, and Simple Tarot Spreads

Runes for Beginners: A Guide to Reading Runes in Divination, Rune Magic, and the Meaning of the Elder Futhark Runes

Wicca Moon Magic: A Wiccan's Guide and Grimoire for Working Magic with Lunar Energies

Wicca Wheel of the Year Magic: A Beginner's Guide to the Sabbats, with History, Symbolism, Celebration Ideas, and Dedicated Sabbat Spells

Wicca Kitchen Witchery: A Beginner's Guide to Magical Cooking, with Simple Spells and Recipes

Wicca Essential Oils Magic: A Beginner's Guide to Working with Magical Oils, with Simple Recipes and Spells

Wicca Elemental Magic: A Guide to the Elements, Witchcraft, and Magical Spells

Wicca Magical Deities: A Guide to the Wiccan God and Goddess, and Choosing a Deity to Work Magic With

Wicca Living a Magical Life: A Guide to Initiation and Navigating Your Journey in the Craft

Magic and the Law of Attraction: A Witch's Guide to the Magic of Intention, Raising Your Frequency, and Building Your Reality

Wicca Altar and Tools: A Beginner's Guide to Wiccan Altars, Tools for Spellwork, and Casting the Circle

Wicca Finding Your Path: A Beginner's Guide to Wiccan Traditions, Solitary Practitioners, Eclectic Witches, Covens, and Circles

Wicca Book of Shadows: A Beginner's Guide to Keeping Your Own Book of Shadows and the History of Grimoires

Modern Witchcraft and Magic for Beginners: A Guide to Traditional and Contemporary Paths, with Magical Techniques for the Beginner Witch

FREE GIFT REMINDER

Just a reminder that Lisa is giving away an exclusive, free spell book as a thank-you gift to new readers!

Little Book of Spells contains ten spells that are ideal for newcomers to the practice of magic, but are also suitable for any level of experience.

Read it on read on your laptop, phone, tablet, Kindle or Nook device by visiting:

www.wiccaliving.com/bonus

DID YOU ENJOY
WICCA WITCHES' PLANNER 2021?

Thanks so much for reading this book! I know there are many great books out there about Wicca, so I really appreciate you choosing this one.

If you enjoyed the book, I have a small favor to ask – would you take a couple of minutes to leave a review for this book on Amazon?

Your feedback will help me to make improvements to this book, and to create even better ones in the future. It will also help me develop new ideas for books on other topics that might be of interest to you. Thanks in advance for your help!

Printed in Great Britain
by Amazon